voices

DIRTY HANDS—PURE HEARTS

SERMONS & CONVERSATIONS WITH HOLINESS PREACHERS

Edited and Compiled by
Tom Nees

BEACON HILL PRESS
OF KANSAS CITY

Printed in the
United States of America

Cover Design: Chad A. Cherry
Cover Photo: Don Pluff
Interior Design: Sharon Page

All Scripture quotations not otherwise designated are from *The Holy Bible, New International-al Version*® (NIV®). Copyright © 1973, 1978, 1984 by International Bible Society. Used by permission of Zondervan Publishing House. All rights reserved.

Permission to quote from the following additional copyrighted versions of the Bible is acknowledged with appreciation:

The *New American Standard Bible*® (NASB®), © copyright The Lockman Foundation 1960, 1962, 1963, 1968, 1971, 1972, 1973, 1975, 1977, 1995.

The *New King James Version* (NKJV). Copyright © 1979, 1980, 1982 Thomas Nelson, Inc.

The *Holy Bible, New Living Translation* (NLT), copyright © 1996. Used by permission of Tyndale House Publishers, Inc., Wheaton, IL 60189. All rights reserved.

The *New Revised Standard Version* (NRSV) of the Bible, copyright 1989 by the Division of Christian Education of the National Council of the Churches of Christ in the USA. Used by permission. All rights reserved.

The Message (TM). Copyright © 1993. Used by permission of NavPress Publishing Group.

Scripture quotations marked KJV are from the King James Version.

Library of Congress Cataloging-in-Publication Data

Dirty hands-pure hearts : sermons and conversations with holiness preachers / edited and compiled by Tom Nees.
    p. cm. — (Voices)
    ISBN 0-8341-2244-8 (pbk.)
    1. Holiness churches—Sermons. 2. Holiness churches—Clergy—Interviews. I. Nees, Thomas G., 1937- II. Series: Voices (Kansas City, Mo.)

BX7990.H6D57 2006
252'.0799—dc22

2006000135

10 9 8 7 6 5 4 3 2 1

CONTENTS

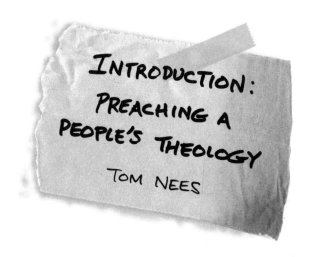

INTRODUCTION: PREACHING A PEOPLE'S THEOLOGY

TOM NEES

The Church of the Nazarene, with its sister holiness denominations, is a message-driven movement. The groups that merged in the early 20th century to form the larger Nazarene family were in general agreement about what is commonly referred to as the Wesleyan-Holiness message—a message shaped by 19th-century Holiness preaching in America.

Mark Quanstrom's *A Century of Holiness Theology** traces the evolution of Holiness thinking in the Church of the Nazarene through two sources —the books approved for studies leading to ordination and changes in the denomination's Articles of Faith approved through the political process of quadrennial assemblies.

Clearly there was, and is, no one individual or authoritative council that has, or can, establish an official, permanent definition of Wesleyan-Holiness theology. While systematic theologians from Richard Watson to H. Orton Wiley have formed a theological context for Holiness theology, the development of Holiness theology also follows the communication of the message through preaching. Holiness theology may be as close as we can come to a people's theology. In the language of computer technology—Holiness theology is an open-source theology with many contributors, both amateur and professional.

In its present form the Holiness message emerged from the preaching and singing of John and Charles Wesley in the 18th-century English evangelical revival. In 19th-century America, Holiness thinking—with its spiritu-

---

*Mark R. Quanstrom, *A Century of Holiness Theology: The Doctrine of Entire Sanctification in the Church of the Nazarene: 1905 to 2004* (Kansas City: Beacon Hill Press of Kansas City, 2004).

al, moral, and social implications—was advanced in a wide variety of camp meetings, prayer groups, and associations of independent congregations.

Even now in the early years of the 21st century the Holiness message is being defined as well as communicated by preacher-theologians, mostly pastors whose sermons evolve from constant dialogue with congregations for whom the Holiness message is a guide for inner spirituality and engagement with the world.

The sermons in this collection were preached by a few well-known preacher-theologians in this tradition. With all their differences, they would all agree with Dr. Sam Vassel in his challenge to Nazarene pastors during the 2004 PALCON conferences, that they are the custodians of a tradition from which the Holiness message evolved and is evolving.

Each sermon in its own way is a commentary on how this message is being passed on to the next generation. Each of these modern-day Holiness preachers expresses his convictions about authenticity in the experience and expression of holiness in personal living and social responsibility. They are anxious to ground the message in the entire biblical record rather than in a few well-known proof texts.

The invitation to participate in this project included the following statement:

> The message of scriptural holiness is about a religious experience. But it is more. It is a worldview. The Wesleyan-Holiness Heritage, as referred to in the Historical Statement in the *Manual of the Church of the Nazarene*, encompasses all the Articles of Faith. It is reflected in the lifestyle guidelines outlined in the Covenant of Christian Conduct—a living and breathing document constantly adapting the life of holiness to a global church in a changing world.

> Understood this way every sermon preached from within the Wesleyan-Holiness Heritage could be thought of as a Holiness sermon. There is a Holiness perspective on social ethics as well as personal conduct. Books have been written about evangelism, leadership, and stewardship in the Wesleyan-Holiness spirit.

> As the Church of the Nazarene enters its second century, this project intends to gather some of the best preaching inspired by the Wesleyan-Holiness movement.

These printed sermons were preached in worship services, a camp meeting, and a compassionate ministry conference and transcribed from tapes. No one sermon could begin to express or even summarize everything a Holiness preacher would like to say about the message. At best, these are samples—but they are good samples, providing insight into the state of preaching by Holiness preacher-theologians today. The brief interviews included before each sermon provide background and context—giving the preachers an opportunity to reflect on how their sermons fit into a lifetime of ministry.

They are formatted to convey the look and feel of a preached sermon rather than an essay—as if eyes could have ears. There is an attempt to preserve the setting, including the personality and idiosyncrasies of the preachers. Regrettably the responses of the congregations—amens, laughter, smiles, tears, and prayers—could not be conveyed adequately on the printed page. The reader will need to insert those using the eyes and ears of the imagination.

1

THESE BROTHERS
& SISTERS
OF MINE
RON BENEFIEL

introduction and interview

Dr. Ron Benefiel, president of Nazarene Theological Seminary in Kansas City (NTS), spent 6 years on staff and then 14 years as pastor of Los Angeles First Church of the Nazarene. Growing up in a parsonage, he began to sense a call to preach during his high school years—a calling he pursued at Pasadena College in San Diego—now Point Loma Nazarene University. After a year of study at NTS he returned to Southern California to serve as his father's youth assistant and at the same time completed a Ph.D. in sociology from the University of Southern California.

In 1996 he began teaching Sociology and Urban Ministry at Point Loma while cofounding the Mid-City Church of the Nazarene, a multicultural urban ministry in San Diego. He was elected president of NTS in 2000.

This sermon was preached at a 1996 conference for leaders of Nazarene Compassionate Ministries in Oklahoma City. He was speaking not so much to but for those who listened. Although he was a university professor at the time, in his sermon he spoke from convictions and conversations developed on the streets of Los Angeles and San Diego during more than 25 years of urban ministry. I asked him about the circumstances in which he came to understand the importance of the Holiness message for urban ministry.

How did your years of ministry on city streets inform this message?

The years of experience in urban ministry shaped my thinking in so many ways, including the way I read Scripture and the way I think about Holiness theology and the ministry of the Church in the world. The ideas and examples that I was drawing from for this message came directly out of my experience of pastoring in Los Angeles.

What does the Wesleyan-Holiness message have to say about human need?

In looking back at our tradition to Wesley and Bresee, I have come to deeply believe that compassion or caring for the poor is not an addendum to our theology of ministry. It's very much tied to holiness, especially the holy character of God. God is holy not only in purity but also in love and compassion, mercy and justice. As the people of God are transformed by the power of God, by the grace of God, and are re-created in God's image, they bear God's holy character in the world. God's love in and through them is a love that engages the world not just in moral purity but also in compassion, mercy, and justice.

How did your training in sociology as well as theology shape your commitment to compassionate ministries?

Those things emerged together. There have been three major shaping influences in my life: Wesleyan-Holiness theology as I've understood and embraced it through the Church of the Nazarene; 25 years of ministry in the city; and graduate-level studies in sociology. The sociology background has helped me understand the world from a different, social-scientific perspective. It has helped me understand how to "exegete" the world, especially with regard to social systems, and has given me a greater awareness of issues related to social justice.

What did you learn from 20 years at Los Angeles First Church?

I learned that from the very beginning the Church of the Nazarene was raised up for two purposes—to proclaim Holiness throughout the land and to minister to and among the poor. I also learned that ministry to and among the poor included ministries not only of compassion but also of social justice. Ministry in the city required us to participate with the poor in ways that allowed us to view the world and the gospel from their perspective.

How did people in your urban congregations respond to this when you preached to them about it?

Rather than preaching to them I saw myself as one with them; we looked to the Word to hear what God had to say to all of us together. At its best, it seemed to be a voice from the Scripture to our shared experience as a pilgrim people in the city—a voice that both challenged us to be Christian in the world and gave us hope that the power of God could actually make us into a Kingdom people.

How did the Holiness message speak to their human experience?

It was mostly implicit. There would have been times, of course, when it would have been explicit. After all, this was the founding church of the Church of the Nazarene. We had a Founders Day every year in which we celebrated the founding of the church usually with messages that specifically focused on Holiness.

Thinking about the implicit, as we reflected on our Nazarene history and Wesleyan theology, much of the Holiness message emerged in ways that continually surprised us as we saw how the holiness of God in compassion, love, and purity serves as a foundation for what it means to be a holy people.

How is the Holiness message viewed at NTS?

You would find the entire faculty to be very committed to the Wesleyan-Holiness message. NTS is a Wesleyan-Holiness seminary that primarily exists to serve the Church of the Nazarene and the larger Wesleyan-Holiness movement. And it's not that in name only—it's that in character, it's that in calling, and it's that in mission. The students who come to NTS are "formed in Christ" in preparation for ministry as they participate in our community. They are formed or shaped for ministry in a community that is committed to Christian Holiness.

You're optimistic about that?

I am. When I think of the Church as being raised up by God and I think of the optimism of grace that is ours as we believe that the Holy Spirit is able to do the transforming work of re-creating us in the image of God, there are lots of reasons to be full of hope.

sermon: "these brothers and sisters of mine"

"But when the Son of Man comes in His glory, and all the angels with Him, then He will sit on His glorious throne. All the nations will be gathered before Him; and He will separate them from one another, as the shepherd separates the sheep from the goats; and He will put the sheep on His right, and the goats on the left. Then the King will say to those on His right,

'Come, you who are blessed of My Father, inherit the kingdom prepared for you from the foundation of the world. For I was hungry, and you gave Me something to eat; I was thirsty, and you gave Me something to drink; I was a stranger, and you invited Me in; naked, and you clothed Me; I was sick, and you visited Me; I was in prison, and you came to Me.'

"Then the righteous will answer Him,

'Lord, when did we see You hungry, and feed You, or thirsty, and give You something to drink? And when did we see You a stranger, and invite You in, or naked, and clothe You? When did we see You sick, or in prison, and come to You?'

"The King will answer and say to them,
   'Truly I say to you, to the extent that you did it to one of these
   brothers of Mine, even the least of them, you did it to Me.'
"Then He will also say to those on His left,
   'Depart from Me, accursed ones, into the eternal fire which has
   been prepared for the devil and his angels; for I was hungry, and
   you gave Me nothing to eat; I was thirsty, and you gave Me nothing to drink; I was a stranger, and you did not invite Me in; naked,
   and you did not clothe Me; sick, and in prison, and you did not
   visit Me.'
"Then they themselves also will answer,
   'Lord, when did we see You hungry, or thirsty, or a stranger, or
   naked, or sick, or in prison, and did not take care of You?'
"Then He will answer them,
   'Truly I say to you, to the extent that you did not do it to one of
   the least of these, you did not do it to Me.'
"These will go away into eternal punishment, but the righteous into
eternal life."

(Matt. 25:31-46, NASB)

Greetings in the name of the Lord!
This is such a good time for me to be with you.
   I miss being with all of you on the streets of our cities.
      Being on the streets in ministry is part of what it means for me to
      be Christian. It is what I understand to be part of my calling to
      serve in the Kingdom—that sense of being present on the margins
      with the poor, with immigrants, with people who are sick or in
      prison, that sense of knowing the grace of God in the margins, wit-
      nessing the Resurrection stories of changed lives through the pow-
      er of God. I miss being there with all of you.
   It seems to me that there isn't any better place to look for revival in
our country and renewal in our church than in the streets and in the
margins of our society.

Even though most of you serve among the poor, you are still, for the
most part, part of the privileged in our world, the blessed with greater access to "power, privilege, and prestige." It's interesting to read Matt. 25 as
people who are the "haves" in our world of great need, isn't it?
   It's a problem of course, when we remember that the U.N. estimates
that every 3.6 seconds somebody in our world starves to death—most-

ly children under the age of five—24,000 people per day, about 1,000 people an hour.

What does it mean to be Christian in that kind of a world—
in our kind of a world?

A lot of Christian folks are talking these days about the end times,
the final day of the Lord's return.

Even though we don't really know for sure, of course,
as Christians we look forward to His soon return.

In Matt. 25 we have three parables of the final day.

Parables about the Lord's return.

You know what they are.

The first one is the parable of the five wise and the five foolish virgins.

What is the message of this parable?

The Lord could return at any time—be ready!

The second parable in this chapter is the parable of the talents.

You remember the story.

One servant had 5 talents and worked hard to increase the number to 10.

Another who had 2 talents worked to increase the number to 4.

And then there was the foolish servant who buried his talent in the ground.

What's the message in this parable?

Well, the king has gone for a while, but the king is coming back.

While the king is away, his servants are to be at work . . .
at work in the things of the kingdom, right?

And then there's this third parable. It's the parable of the sheep and the goats.

What's the third parable say? Ahh, this is interesting! Let's take a look.

The first thing we notice is that there are some surprises in this passage.

Just thinking about the end times and the return of the Lord,
I think my normal response would be,
"Wow! You know, if it's getting toward the end, we need to get everybody saved and ready to go into heaven. We need to have the biggest evangelistic campaign we've ever had!"

And, of course, I think we should do just that.

But when I read this parable, I'm surprised at what I find.

The message of these parables is
first—"Be ready,"
second—"Be at work in the Kingdom,"
and third, get this—*"Care for the poor!"*

Why would Jesus, when He is talking about the day of His return, instruct His disciples to put time and effort and energy into caring for the poor? Wouldn't it make more sense if He instructed them to invest all their time and energy in evangelism?

Isn't this a surprise?

There are other surprises in this passage as well.

For example, there is a common theme running through these three parables regarding God's judgment. In all three parables, people are judged not for things they have done, for sins they committed, but instead for things they didn't do!

The five foolish virgins are shut out of the Kingdom because they *didn't have oil in their lamps.*

And the wicked steward is refused entrance because he hid his talent in the ground—

He didn't do *anything!*

He buried his talent in the ground, knowing that when the master would come the master would demand of him an accounting. And he wanted to make sure he didn't lose it. So *he didn't do anything with it.*

He was judged to be a wicked servant—*for doing nothing!*

And here in the last parable, the goats who are judged are judged not for what they did—

but, again, for what they didn't do.

They didn't feed the hungry or visit those who were sick or in prison.

They were judged for what they did not do! That's a surprise, isn't it?

When I look further at this third parable,

perhaps the biggest surprise of all are the looks on the faces of the people in the final day . . .

both the sheep and the goats.

Here's a picture of the great and final day of the Lord,

and here is King Jesus who has returned,

and He separates the sheep from the goats—

the sheep on His right and the goats on His left.

And He looks to the sheep on His right and says,

"Come, you who are blessed of My Father, inherit the kingdom prepared for you from the foundation of the world. For I was hungry, and you gave Me something to eat; I was thirsty, and you gave Me something to drink; I was a stranger, and you invited Me in; . . . I was in prison, and you came to Me" (Matt. 25:34-36).

And on the faces of the righteous we see this picture of surprise.

It's as though they are saying,

"You mean there were other people who didn't care for those in need? Isn't caring for the poor just what we were supposed to do as Christians?

Isn't it what we do because it is who we are as followers of Christ?"

And then there is a similar surprise on the faces of the goats on the left who didn't help those in need.

We see the surprise on their faces as if they are saying,

"What? Really?" "That was You, Lord? That was You?

We didn't know that was You there among the poor!

Why didn't You tell us that was You?"

I've been thinking about this picture of surprise, especially on the faces of the righteous . . .

and the nature of the character of holiness.

"Holiness" is the word more than any other word that describes the whole of the character of God. Usually when we have thought about holiness in our tradition, we've especially thought of it in terms of the "holy otherness" and purity of God—the moral purity of God. And, of course, holiness is that. God is holy other, spotless and pure. But as we think of holiness as the whole character of God—the character of God in holiness describes not only God's purity but also God's love and God's mercy. So to speak of God's holiness is also to speak of God's compassion. To speak of the character of God, the holiness of God, is also to speak of God's justice, His care for the poor, His love for all people as all are created in His image. So the holiness of God encompasses more than just the moral purity of God. It is the whole of the love of God, the justice of God, the mercy of God, and the compassion of God.

We also have come to understand that the grace of God re-creates in us, restores in us, the image of God—and *we become by the power of the grace of God, the holy people of God!* Being the holy people of God is not just being removed from the world; it is not just being morally pure. But as the holy character of God is re-created in the people of God, the love of God, the mercy of God, the compassion of God, and the justice of God are reproduced and exhibited in the people of God. The holy character of God is expressed in the people of God so that the whole world ought to be able to look at the people of God and see something of the holy character of God.

The Church, then, is the prophetic witness in the world of what the kingdom of God will look like when Christ returns. Again, the whole world ought to be able to look at the people of God and see something about the "already-not yet" Kingdom. As Christians, we bear not only the name of Christ but the character of Christ as well. The people of God through their lives give testimony to who God is—*who we are speaks of God in the world!*

In Matt. 25, Jesus describes for us what that looks like as the righteous ones feed the hungry, visit the sick, and care for those in need.

Henri Nouwen writes—I love this—he says,
"Wherever true Christian community is formed, compassion happens in the world" *(Compassion: A Reflection on the Christian Life)*.
Ha! Don't you like that? Listen to it again,
"Wherever true Christian community is formed, compassion happens in the world."
That's the holy people of God—out of their new nature in Christ Jesus—acting in love and compassion for the poor. *It is what we do because of who we are in Christ Jesus!*

This parable is one that keeps talking to us. Every time I look at this passage there's more. There are four words in particular that emerge from this passage for me:

The first word is **stewardship.** In reading these words of Jesus, the straightforward message is that we are to give to those in need and to help those in distress. Christian stewardship takes it a step further in challenging us not only to contribute to the needs of the poor but also to think of our resources as God's—to be used as God intends.

John Wesley had some things to say about this. For Wesley, there are two ways that Christians think about money. The first is to think in terms of God's blessings. God has blessed us and placed in our hands a certain amount of wealth. And because God has blessed us with this wealth, we should be thankful. Further, we are indebted to God for His great gift, and what we owe God in return is thanks—thanks to God for what He has given to us.

This is what we celebrate at Thanksgiving, isn't it?
In this American society we think back about how God has blessed us individually, and blessed our families, and blessed our country.

We take a day and give thanks to God for what He has given us—
for His abundance and blessing.
And we wonder sometimes why God hasn't blessed some other folks,
too,
but we figure we can't really control that.
That's God's business.
Maybe they weren't as diligent in responding to the grace of God
or something. But they didn't get blessed.
And that's sort of their problem.
Of course, we ought to give a little extra to those in need . . .
out of our abundance,
doling out a little to help out some of those that are lagging be-
hind.
But it's not really our responsibility . . .
it is a symbol of our *generosity,* not our *responsibility.*
It's their responsibility—and God's—but not really ours.
This is not John Wesley's perspective on wealth.
For Wesley, money—wealth—is never really ours at all.
It is always God's.
It's never actually given to us. It's only entrusted to our care. We are
never the owners.
We don't owe God thanks for what He has given us.
Instead we owe God everything. All we have is His . . .
the complete, absolute, full consecration of all we are and all we have
in response to God's loving invitation to surrender ourselves fully in-
to His hands.
So that the driving response to God's love and call on our lives
is not so much one of giving thanks alone,
although certainly we should have a thankful spirit,
but rather to continually ask the question,
"Lord, what is it that You want done with what is Yours?
What do You want me to do with Your money,
Your resources,
with this life that is now fully Yours?
What is it You want done with what is Yours?"
Wesley is really quite radical about this.
To tell you the truth, it's more radical than I'm comfortable with.
And I'll tell you right now, it's probably going to be more radical than
you're comfortable with too.

For Wesley, the definition of wealth was anything beyond the bare necessities of survival—

food, clothing, and shelter.

For Wesley, all the money Christians had beyond the bare necessities
had been entrusted by God to their care for the purpose of giving to
those in need.

And if you used any of those "extra" resources on yourself,

you were *robbing from God and the poor!*

For Wesley, the reason God gave you these resources—this money, this
time, this talent—

(or should I say, entrusted them to your care?)

was so that you could use them to accomplish God's purposes
as a steward of what belongs to God.

And what does God want done with what is His?

God has entrusted these resources into your hands to help
those in need.

Whew! I told you, you wouldn't like it!

At one point, a member of the early Methodist movement wrote Wesley
with a question. Essentially, the question was, "I have received this extra
money and I've already given to the poor and I've already paid my tithe,
and I have this special thing that I want to get for myself. Is there any
problem with that?" It's the old you-owe-it-to-yourself motif. Listen to
Wesley's response:

"Perhaps you say you can now *afford* the expense. This is . . . nonsense.
Who gave you this wealth; or (to speak properly) *lent* it to you? To
speak more properly still, who lodged it for a time in your hands as
his stewards; informing you at the same time for what purposes he
entrusted you with it? And can you *afford* to waste your Lord's goods?
. . . Away with this vile, diabolical cant! . . . This *affording* to rob God is
the very cant of hell. Do not you know that God entrusted you with
that money (all above what buys necessities for your families), that
God entrusted you with that money to feed the hungry, to clothe the
naked, to help the stranger, the widow, the fatherless; and, indeed as
far as it will go, to relieve the wants of all mankind?"

(Sermon 126, "On the Danger of Increasing Riches," in *Sermons on
Several Occasions*)

Strong words—if we give an altar call right now, I'd have to be the first
one to come to the altar.

I wrestle with all of this, a lot.

In the middle of this, I hear the voice of God calling us . . .

calling us away from merely giving thanks to God for what we have,
> to understanding that we are stewards of God's resources
>> and that everything we have and everything we are belongs to God.

And again, the question is, "Lord, what is it You want done with what is Yours?"

The second word that emerges from this parable for me is the word **presence.**

As I look at this passage, I see that the sheep, those who were the righteous,
> not only gave to the poor
>> *but also were present with the poor.*

In the parable, Jesus says,
> "I was hungry, and *you gave Me something to eat.*
> I was thirsty, and *you gave Me something to drink.*
> I was sick and in prison, and *you came to visit Me"* (see Matt. 25:35-36).
>> Now, I think we all ought to send everything we can to Nazarene Compassionate Ministries or Compassion International, since we all can't go where they can go to serve among the poor.

But part of what Jesus calls us to in this parable is to go . . .
> to be there personally,
>> to be present among the poor.
> You visited Me. You came to Me in prison. You clothed Me.
>> You were there.
> You didn't just read about the plight of the poor; you didn't just send money.
> You were there.

I used to teach at Point Loma Nazarene University.

> It's a wonderful school in almost every way you can imagine.

Sometimes at Point Loma, there would be a discussion describing the campus as being something of a "bubble,"
> somehow removed from the real world—a sort of artificial place.

In one of the courses I taught every year, I would take the students with me to visit Los Angeles.
> We'd visit the barrio and the ghetto and contrast it with a visit to Rodeo Drive.

We'd visit Scott Chamberlain and the Central City Community Church on skid row.

All this, of course, was unsettling to the students. The contrast of life in "the bubble" and the streets of Los Angeles was destabilizing in a way that it created what psychologists call cognitive dissonance for the students. Such dissonance was noted by one student, Mark, who submitted the following article to the school newspaper after returning from one of our visits to Los Angeles. An edited portion of the article is as follows:

> "Friday night I walked the slums of L.A., specifically skid row. . . . Until you've stepped around the cardboard boxes, smelled the scent of trash and urine that filled the street, or looked into the eyes of the homeless, . . . you can't even begin to understand the tragedy of destitution in the city. . . .

> "[Later], I walked up and down Rodeo Drive. I watched the police harass an innocent homeless man who just happened to be standing by himself drinking Jamba Juice, just the same as the dozen wealthier people around him. [I felt ashamed and left] with feelings of anger. . . .

> "Sunday, I was back in skid row attending church. . . . For the first time I was the minority, I was the different one. But they welcomed me. They showed me love. They taught me a lesson about what it really means to be a Christian. They were the same faces from Friday night. And they were raising their arms and crying out to God with a level of passion that I could never comprehend. For them, worship was a time of liberation and freedom from a world that has left them for dead. . . . Their faith is real."

Being personally present isn't just for the benefit of those we are there to help. Being present among the poor challenges our givens and helps us see things from a different perspective—perhaps you might even say from a Kingdom perspective. The movement of the Kingdom is incarnational. It is a movement that follows Jesus into the world. It is a movement that calls us, with Jesus, to be personally present among the poor, to take up our residence among those in need.

Henri Nouwen writes,

> "Here we see what compassion means. It is not a bending toward the underprivileged from a privileged position. It is not a reaching out from on high to those who are less fortunate below. It is not a gesture of sympathy or pity for those who fail to make it in the upward pull.

On the contrary, compassion means going directly to those people
and places where suffering is most acute and building a home there"
(Compassion: A Reflection on the Christian Life).

So the words that emerge from this parable are
"stewardship"—serving as stewards of God's resources to care for the poor,
   "presence"—being there personally,
      and the third word—**hospitality.**
It's interesting to read this passage and hear in it the language of hospi-
tality.
   Listen again:
   "I was hungry, and you gave Me something to eat; I was thirsty, and
   you gave Me something to drink; I was a stranger, and you invited Me
   in" (Matt. 25:35, NASB).
This is in the language of hospitality—isn't it?
Let's take this a step further.
One of the ways to talk about the grace of God is also in the language of
hospitality.
   (I've heard Reuben Welch talk about this, so I have it on pretty good
   authority!)
God in His grace makes room for us, invites us into His own space.
   As Christians, we talk a lot about Christ in us (the hope of glory).
      But it is also true that we are in Christ (as the branches are in the
      vine).
   He invites us into himself—to be partakers of His divine nature.
Here we are in our sinfulness and our ignorance and our crazy theologies,
   and He makes space for us.
God is long-suffering and compassionate and just—but He is also merci-
ful.
   God graciously welcomes us into himself—
      He makes space for us, room for us. He has patience with us.
   The grace of God is in this sense the hospitality of God.
   And we are called to have the same attitude, the same spirit, that is in
   Christ Jesus.
We are ones who have known the grace, the forgiveness, the hospitality of
God.
   As we have freely received, we are called to freely give.
   For us to be hospitable, for us to be as grace-giving as we have been
   grace-receiving,

is to welcome others into our lives. To welcome the poor, the hungry,
those who don't think or talk or smell or look the way we would prefer.
But as we have known the grace of God in all of our own sinful ugliness and ignorance,
we now as the holy people of God extend the hospitality of God
to the poor, to the people of our world, to the lost and the broken
—*extending hospitality as grace and grace as hospitality.*

Tim started coming to the church I pastored in Los Angeles. There he found Jesus. I met him on the street sometime shortly after his conversion. I still remember his words; he said,

"I don't know if you know about me, about who I really am, about my past. I have spent most of my life in bars." He said, "I've been married 10 times, and I can't ever remember actually getting married. I was usually drunk. I just remember usually waking up the next morning and discovering that I was married!" He said, "I've totaled about 25 cars. I'm just a drunk"

And then he said,

"I can't believe that the people at the church have welcomed me in.
I never thought I could be accepted by respectable folks."
(And I thought about the rest of us in the congregation and wondered what
"respectable folks" he was talking about!)

Tim moved away some time after that. I kept track of him. He got involved in a church in the community where he moved. Years later, he was still serving God. His life had been changed by the grace of God. Not just because God reached out and found him but because the people of God that I had the privilege of being a part expressed the grace of God to him by welcoming him into their fellowship—a community of Christians where he knew the love of God because the people of God expressed God's grace and love to him and welcomed him in.

Let me briefly tell you another story. A story about a man named Douglas Sowers.

As you know, sometimes elderly people move into the city because that's where they can access the services they need for basic survival. And that's where they sometimes go to die.

In our neighborhood in Los Angeles, there were a lot of big 40-unit hotels—old four-story brick masonry buildings that would be the first ones to cave in if we had a big earthquake. A group of us decided we wanted to make contact with some of those who lived in the hotels, so we organized ourselves into what we called the Neighborhood Christian Service Corp. We would meet and divide up by twos, and then we'd go calling. Two of us would take on one of those big old brick apartment buildings as our ministry. And we'd go door-to-door and hand out a flyer that would identify who we were. Typically, we would knock on the doors of the apartment units, hand out the flyers, and say, "We're Christians from the neighborhood. Is there anything you need that we can help you with? We'll be back next week."

One day, Ruth, my ministry partner and I, knocked on the door of Douglas Sowers (pronounced "Sours"). His last name was actually pretty descriptive of his voice. I remember when we knocked on his door the first time, we heard this screechy, crotchety voice respond; we couldn't really tell if it was an old man or an old woman. He didn't open the door. He peeked out through the crack in the barely opened door and said,

"I-I don't really want to talk to anybody."

I said, "We're from the church."

He said, "Well, I don't-I don't really want to talk to anybody from the church."

We said, "Well, we'll be back next week."

We came back the next week. This time when he came to the door, he said,

"Well, I guess you can come in, but I don't want anything from the church."

We came back every week and started getting to know Douglas, and about what his life was like.

We discovered he lived alone and never had any personal contact with anybody.

Not anybody!

His neighbors knew he was alive because every morning when they were done with their newspaper, they would put it in front of his door for him. And when he was finished with it, he'd put it in front of some other neighbor's door. But they never talked with one another.

He had no contact with anybody.

In 10 years, he hadn't been more than two blocks from his apartment— just far enough to get to the local store and back.

His television was on 24 hours a day. The sound of the TV kept him company.

It was the closest thing he had to a friend.

Douglas Sowers—an old man in the city waiting to die.

Ruth, my ministry partner, was a librarian.

On one of our visits she asked Douglas if he liked to read.

And he said, "Sure."

And she said, "Well, how about if I bring you some books next week?"

And so the next week she brought Douglas a whole stack of books—some of the great classics. We came back the week after that, and we asked,

"Douglas, did you have a chance to read any of the books?"

And he said, "Yeah, I read 'em all!"

So we brought him some more books, and he read those too.

Shortly after that when we came for our weekly visit, Douglas said,

"Would it be OK if I went to church with you Sunday?"

And we said, "Sure."

That Sunday night we picked him up and he came to church with us. At the end of the service I saw him in the back standing all alone with a great big tear running down the side of his face.

I came up to him and said, "Douglas, what's wrong?"

And he said, "Oh, nothin'—

I just didn't know there were this many friendly people in the whole world!"

We have known God's gracious hospitality.

What a privilege to be graciously hospitable to others!

Do you know how sometimes you can be present but not really welcoming or hospitable?

Do you know how you can offer a food program through your church, but not really be grace giving?

You know where you're doing the food distribution, but you're not really welcoming—you're not allowing people into your life.

You're not including—you're not inviting. You're just distributing services.

You know what I'm saying?

Here is this word that emerges out of Matt. 25. It says that the righteous were there personally with the poor—and invited them in, in a spirit of hospitality.

I have one more word to suggest to you out of this passage. It is the word **compassion**.

(I prefer the word "solidarity," but I suppose "compassion" is more easily understood.)
The word "compassion" includes the idea of being "one with,"
    especially being one with people in their suffering.
In this passage Jesus says, "Inasmuch as you did it to one of the least of these My brethren" (v. 40, NKJV).
    It's interesting that He doesn't say "the least of these My *subjects,* or My *servants.*"
        But rather, it's "the least of these My brethren."
Jesus identifies those in need as His brothers.
And further He says,
    "Inasmuch as you did it to one of the least of these My brethren,
        you did it to Me" (NKJV).
    Jesus is there with them—one with them, one of them!
One of those in need who are cared for by the righteous is none other than Jesus!
    He is so much with the people in the margins, the lost, those in need
        that He knows fully what it means to be hungry with the hungry,
            sick with the sick, thirsty with the thirsty,
                and poor with the poor.
This gives us additional insight into passages like the ones in which Jesus saw the crowd dejected like sheep without a shepherd and felt *compassion* for them.
    Or images in the New Testament when the blind, the paralyzed, and the deaf
        were being brought to Him, and He felt *compassion* for them.
    Or the two blind men who called out after Him, and He felt *compassion* for them.
    Or the leper who fell to his knees in front of Jesus and said,
        "If You are willing, You can make me clean" (Matt. 8:2, NKJV).
        And He felt *compassion* for him.
    Or the widow who was burying her only son—and He felt *compassion* for her.

This is a compassion that comes from being "present with" those in need.
    It is a compassion that, with Jesus, feels the pain of those who are on the margins,
        those who are the poor, those who are the lost, those who are the hungry,
            because we are there with them.

This kind of compassion changes us.
It leads us to think and pray differently, to live differently.

For me, one of the great privileges of pastoring was the privilege of praying the pastoral prayer.

Sometimes during the pastoral prayer as people would come forward,
I would go down and stand next to those who were praying
and, as their pastor, lay hands on them and pray for them.

I can still see all this very clearly:

Over on this end of the altar is John. Every Sunday he's at the altar. John is an alcoholic. Well, he hasn't had anything to drink in several years, but he knows he's an alcoholic. And every Sunday he comes to the altar to thank God for his sobriety—every Sunday!

"Dear Lord, thank You for John. Bless him.
We give You thanks for another week, another day to be sober and alive in You!"

And here next to John is Royce and his wife, Julie, who received word from the doctors that the baby Julie was carrying probably wouldn't live. And if by some strange turn of events, the baby should live, he would be deformed. And the doctors suggested the possibility of the baby being aborted. And Royce and Julie replied, "No, we want to go full-term with this child." And the church prayed. And the baby was born and named Spencer. And today he's 11 years old—a happy, healthy boy! And as they kneel at the altar, they are giving thanks for their son, Spencer. And all of us together are reassured of the love and power of God and give glory and thanks for God's miraculous works!

But a little further down the altar I see Sylvester and Yuri. And in the sixth month of Yuri's pregnancy, Yuri had a miscarriage. I still remember the cold day I went out onto a hill in a cemetery where Sylvester and Yuri stood next to a tiny little casket, praying for the grace and comfort of God.

And here at the altar is Harry, and Stanley is kneeling next to him. They both came to the Lord later in life. Harry was in his 50s and Stanley's in his 60s. Harry was a wild man in most every respect before coming to Christ. But now in his new life in Christ, he has a wonderful gift of evangelism. He keeps bringing people to Jesus. And Stanley is one of those who Harry just brought to the Lord. And here they are at the altar, praying together and giving thanks to God for Stanley's newfound life in Christ Jesus!

And on down the altar, there is Meselu. She's from Ethiopia. She's here in the U.S. alone. She was the one chosen by her family to come to the U.S. to establish residency in hopes that the rest of the family could follow. So she left her husband and four small children behind and has been eking out a living in the tough ghettos of downtown Los Angeles for two years. And she's praying for her family today, longing for them, hoping they are all right, praying that she will be able to see them again soon.

Do you know what it means to be a pastor and the privilege of being present with, hospitable toward, one with the people you pastor?
    What a great privilege!
And when we are one with those in need, we pray differently.
We pray differently for the poor and the broken.
    We pray differently for immigrants and the homeless.
      We pray differently for the elderly.
      And we pray differently for children.

Also, when we are one with those in need, we must realize that Jesus is already there in the midst. Wherever there are poor in the world, wherever there are people in need, Jesus is already there among them. We do not bring Jesus with us.
    Rather, He calls us to come join Him among the poor and needy. Mother Teresa said,
    "I know that when I touch the limbs of a leper who stinks I am touching the body of Christ the same as when I receive the Sacrament. This conviction of touching Christ under the appearance of a leper gives me a courage which I would not have otherwise. Today once more, Jesus comes among His own, and His own do not know Him. He comes in the hurt bodies of our poor. Jesus comes to you and me, and often, very often, we let Him pass without noticing" *(A Gift for God: Prayers and Meditations)*.

In this passage, Jesus calls us to follow Him to love and care for those in need,
    to know their pain as our own.
These four words are words to remember from this parable:
    The call to **stewardship**—to give, remembering that everything we have belongs to God.
    The call to be **present**—to be physically, personally present among those we serve.
    The call to be **hospitable**—to welcome the poor into our lives, to make room for them,

to be grace-giving as we ourselves have known the grace of God.
And the call to **compassion**—to be one with, to feel with,
to know the pain of those in need in our world as our own.

Henri Nouwen writes,
"Radical servanthood challenges us . . .
to reveal the gentle presence . . .
of our compassionate God . . .
in the midst of our broken world" *(Compassion: A Reflection on the Christian Life).*
Thanks be to God!

2

**DIRTY HANDS—
PURE HEARTS**

DAN BOONE

introduction and interview

I interviewed Dr. Dan Boone soon after he had been elected president of Trevecca Nazarene University (Nashville). He was in his final days as pastor of the Olivet College Church of the Nazarene in Bourbonnais, Illinois. He has been preaching since his early teens and was appointed to his first pastorate near his home in Macomb, Mississippi, when he was a high school junior. After graduating from Trevecca in 1974 and Nazarene Theological Seminary in 1977, he went on to pastor churches in Raleigh, North Carolina, and Nashville before going to his pastorate at College Church. He has also served as a preaching professor at Nazarene Theological Seminary.

I asked him about his development as a Holiness preacher.

Growing up in Mississippi, I had the sense that Nazarene folk were not quite up to par with all the other denominations and that maybe our theology was a little off to the side somewhere. It was Bill Greathouse at NTS who showed me we could stand with the saints of the ages and speak our message. It was mainstream, it was deeply biblical, and it had historical roots that we should never be ashamed of. And I think we haven't even to this day claimed our roots as proudly as we ought to.

What do your years of rich pastoral experience teach you about being a university president?

I take with me the understanding that the regional university has a responsibility to look in two directions. It has to look to the churches that are sending their students to the university. And it has to talk about what the university is and does and how that gives hope to the local congregations—that their students might ex-

29

*perience a holy calling and be sent back to the churches as trained and equipped
servants ready to meet the need for God in the world.*

How did you react when notified that you had been elected president of
your alma mater?

*When they told me on a Friday morning, "You've been elected president," I
thought, "Oh my, I've got some praying to do." I picked up the phone and called
a couple of my mentors—Bill Greathouse and Ray Dunning. I wanted to know if
a Holiness preacher could be the president of a university in a complex, technolog-
ical, higher education world like the one we have today. Both of them said that
the primary role of the president of a university is to turn the story of that university into the story of God for the sake of the local church. And the more I listened
and thought about that, the more this seemed to be for me the next chapter in
my ministry. And the last thing in the world I want to do is lay down my identity
as a Holiness preacher as I move toward being a university president.*

In your sermon from the Beatitudes you redefine the common understanding of purity.

*Yes, yes I do. And one of the things I think that happened between Judaism and
the Gospels in New Testament language and literature was that purity for the
Pharisees quite easily became separation from the unclean. But in the Gospel stories we read of Jesus beginning to break the barriers between the clean and unclean. And while the Pharisees viewed holiness as barriers of separation, Jesus
seemed to identify the holy love of God as penetrating those barriers. He was willing to associate with the unclean, bringing the gospel to the poor and those
deemed sinners by both occupation and the law of purity. I sense that our own denomination is on the mission of God when our hands are dirty, when we're focus-
ing on what it means to get our hands dirty, crossing those kinds of barriers in the
name of Jesus to offer the gospel of forgiveness and grace and justice and compassion to the poor, to those who are on the other side of those kinds of lines.*

In your sermon you tell a wonderful story about your uncle Harley.

*Yeah. His smoking habit landed him on the wrong side of the line. And he would
have been labeled in New Testament terms impure because of that habit. And
yet I saw in his life a depth of love for the hobos that came to his front door—a
depth of love driven by his relationship with God. Now in no way am I suggesting
that we ought to change our standard about smoking, that we ought to call people to a less-than-great stewardship of their bodies. But I think sometimes we so
categorize those kinds of behaviors that it makes us smug on a side of the line
where caring for hobos is not mandatory. It may be what Jesus meant when He
said that the sinners and prostitutes and tax collectors would enter the kingdom
of heaven more quickly than the righteous rulers of the Law, that those who see*

life as love toward the needy are much closer to the kingdom of God than those that try to draw some kind of an imaginary line to keep themselves from being defiled by people like that.

Do Holiness people agree with this definition of purity?

After 14 years as pastor here at Olivet College Church, people thank me for opening their eyes to the world around us here in Kankakee County, for opening the church to all kinds of people. And now the church is filled with all kinds of people that had never darkened the door before, and probably would not have darkened the door before—because now we welcome them with a gracious hospitality, and we're willing to get our hands dirty in the middle of their messes. The Pharisees never would have run a church like this. They would have sent a very quiet but strong message that said, "You're an outsider, and you're an insider." And I think the ministry of Jesus begins to penetrate those kinds of barriers.

And how would the people in your congregation describe holiness in their own lives?

I think they would describe it as holy love—the willingness to love the unlovable —the expression of compassion, mercy, and grace in the midst of the world. They would describe it as a Christlikeness that is willing to befriend the kind of people that Jesus befriended. I think they would describe it as a "loving of the enemy" and a "seeking of reconciliation with the enemy." I think they would pick it up and define it in those kinds of terms.

What about the so-called standards that define holy living?

The moralistic issues of smoking, drinking, entertainment, and other such things involve us in making missionally effective choices. We care for our bodies because we want to be healthy pictures of Christlikeness—of people who love our neighbors as ourselves. Therefore, it requires some level of self-love and self-stewardship to be able to do that. So we say no to those things that would hinder our mission of being Christlike in the world. I think the Holiness Movement has often been more concerned with its own image—"How do we look? "How does the world see us?" It's a self-absorbed concern. I don't think Jesus cared about how He looked to the world. I don't think He was trying to project a particular kind of image. I think the concern of Jesus was to see the world correctly.

What can Holiness people do to preserve their message?

I think we need to give our life away. In many ways we are more concerned about preserving our institutions than we are about serving our world. If we go out of business giving our life away in serving the world around us and its needs—if we go out of business doing that, we will have taken on the cruciform of Jesus. It's exactly what Jesus did. He so gave His life away that He went out of business on a cross, taking the last dying face that wanted help with Him into eternity. The Ho-

liness message is best preserved by giving our lives away in service to the world. And I think the more we are concerned with preserving ourselves, the more we fall into the trap Jesus was trying to get His own followers out of when He said, "Those who want to save their life will lose it, and those who lose their life for my sake . . . will save it" (Mark 8:35, NRSV).

How do you feel about the present generation of seminary students?
I have more optimism today than I've ever had about the kind of Holiness preachers that Nazarene Theological Seminary is sending out into our churches. They're good preachers! They know how to tell the story. They understand the Holiness message, and I think they're excited about it. I walk away from every one of those classes wishing I were 20 to 25 again, because we've got great Holiness preachers on the way through our seminary.

sermon: "dirty hands—pure hearts"

The Beatitudes have often been misunderstood as a description of what we should strive to be. They're not that at all. The Beatitudes are the roll call of people about to be blessed by the arrival of a new kingdom. Today, we come to verse 8. And the Word of the Lord says,

"Blessed are the pure in heart, for they will see God" (Matt. 5:8, NRSV).

Words have different meanings, depending on when and where they're spoken.

Take the word "Ohio." Any other time, it would have meant a state east of here. But to speak the word "Ohio" in a week when the presidential election was decided there means something more.

Take the word "homecoming." It's a generic word that can be plugged into a lot of places. But for many of you who are here today at Olivet's annual homecoming, it means something very specific.

Take the word "pure." It's in our beatitude. This is one of those words that changes meaning based on when and where it's spoken. So I find myself asking, "What did Jesus mean when He spoke this particular beatitude: 'Blessed are the pure in heart, for they will see God'?"

One of the responsibilities of preachers is to build a bridge from the world of the text—the social, cultural world of the text—to the world where all of us live. When we hear the word "pure," we're already thinking about what that word means and how we might interpret it, especially in the context of a Nazarene congregation with our doctrines of holiness and sanctification and cleansing and purity. But what did "pure" mean when and where it was spoken?

I'd like to take you to the world of this beatitude for a few moments. I think you'll be very interested in what the word "pure" meant for Jesus and those who listened in Matthew's crowd that day.

The social and cultural world in Jesus' day was governed by a purity system. They had a purity patrol. And I imagine they had those little marker gadgets like those used by the Wal-Mart discounters who walk up to an item and shoot a label on it. But the leaders of Bible times had only two labels. One of the labels read "pure," and the other label read "impure." And the purity patrol would walk around the people, places, and things and label it either pure or impure. This was the cultural measuring tool of that day; it said what was in bounds and what was out of bounds, what was fair and what was foul, clean and unclean. This was the way of the day in which Jesus spoke.

Now I know that you—had you lived in that day—you're the kind of crowd that would definitely be labeled pure. But to be certain about it, let me tell you what it would take for you to be labeled pure.

Your family of origin would have a lot to do with it. If you were born of a Jewish priestly family, a Levitical family, a pure-blood Israelite family, you had a good chance of being labeled pure. But if you were a half-breed Samaritan, you would get the impure label. And if you were a Gentile, you would definitely get the impure label. So most of us in this room are in trouble to start with. Your family of origin had a lot to do with your purity.

Your work had a lot to do with it. If you happened by occupation to be a tender of sheep or pigs, or if you worked in the military—especially during the Roman occupation—or if you were a tax collector or a prostitute, you belonged to a group that automatically was labeled "impure." It was not necessarily a moral thing being said about you—it was just where you stood in light of the purity patrol. And if you held one of these unclean jobs, then you were marked impure. Your vocation had a lot to do with it.

Your friends, your acquaintances, the people you hang around with—they would have a lot to do with whether you're marked pure or impure. Some of the people you eat with—they would get you marked impure because you may be eating with the tax collector. I mean, you could be from a pure-bred Jewish family—you could be a Levitical person—your family tree could be perfect, and yet here you are eating with this tax collector, so you get the label "impure." Who you ate with and hung around with had a lot to do with which label was placed on you.

Your body had a lot to do with being pure. And I know most of you have perfect bodies. But if you were born (let's just say, "What if?") if you were born missing a finger, or with some kind of handicap—if you could not see, if you could not hear, if you had a skin disease, if you had open sores, if there was any sort of handicap about you—if you were less than a *perfect* human specimen, you would be labeled "impure."

Your wealth had a lot to do with it. Now if you were rich—well, that goes a long way toward deserving the pure label. Because the assumption was if you're rich, then God has favored you. He must like you a lot. But you could be wealthy and a Samaritan, and being a half-breed Samaritan would certainly trump being wealthy. So being wealthy didn't automatically mean you were pure, but it helped a lot. Being poor pretty much guaranteed that you were going to be impure, because people who were poor couldn't afford the required sacrifices and they had to work the kind of jobs that were left for those at the bottom of the social class. And you know their vocation was probably going to be bad. So if you were poor, you didn't have very much chance of being pure.

Beyond this, if your family of origin has not disqualified you, if your body or your wealth or your job or your friends have not disqualified you, gender might well do it, because men had a whole lot easier time being pure than women did. Bleeding made a woman impure for certain periods of time. Men were viewed as pure more often than women.

This is how that world ran—pure-impure. Family of origin, vocation, friendships, dinner companions, physical health, net worth, gender—these are a lot of things we don't have a whole lot of choice about. And to assure that this purity system remained in force there was always the purity patrol, the Pharisees who went around with their labeling guns, making sure that nothing was mistaken for pure that was actually impure.

Had the Pharisees been announcing the Beatitudes, we would have heard, "Blessed are the men of pure-bred birth, who are specimens of pure health, who are employed in clean work, who are endowed with wealth and are observant of the purity laws. Blessed are these because they will see God." These Pharisees were the gatekeepers enabling a person to get to where God is. And the Pharisees were always on purity patrol.

But one day in time—it's right here in the Gospel of Matthew—one day in time Jesus went up the mountain and His disciples and the crowds came to Him. And He saw them and He sat down, like a king on a throne. And He began to make kingly pronouncements that a new sheriff was in town, a new reign had come into the world, a new kingdom was being established. And He began to bless groups of people that hadn't been blessed before. And what Jesus said was not, "Blessed are those who are pure born, pure bodied, pure 'vocationed,' and pure gendered."
He didn't say that. He said,

"Blessed are the pure in heart" (5:8, NRSV).

And I'm telling you, this was good news. This was good news for everybody who wasn't born right or whose body didn't function well or whose job got his or her hands dirty. This was good news for all those folks that day. Blessings—the kingdom of heaven is for the likes of these.

I find it interesting what happens at the end of the sermon. You see the verses at the end of chapter 7? Jesus has finished speaking to the crowds and in verse 28 of chapter 7, it says:

"When Jesus had finished saying these things, the crowds were astounded at his teaching, for he taught them as one having authority, and not as their scribes" (NRSV).

The people are concluding that in this new kingdom—under this new rule, in this whole new social order breaking into the world—Jesus has the authority to take the labeling gun away from the purity patrol and to call clean whatever He wants to call clean, and dirty whatever He wants to call dirty.

I know this because of the next two chapters in Matthew's Gospel. Scroll with me down through these two chapters. Look at the list of people that Jesus begins to see and touch and hang around with, and you tell me what is common about this parade of people.

In chapter 8, verse 1 you find that He cleanses a leper. In verse 3 it says, "He stretched out his hand and touched him, saying, '. . . Be made clean!'" (NRSV). He touched the skin-diseased man.

In verse 5, you find the story of a centurion from Capernaum, one whose vocation makes him unclean. And Jesus talks to him about healing a servant back home, and the guy says, "You don't have to come to my house." That would have also made Jesus unclean. Well, Jesus is already unclean because He's associating with a person of unclean vocation. But He goes on to tell this man that his faith is actually greater than any other faith found among the pure-bred Israelites. This does not sit well with the purity patrol, I'm telling you.

Look down at verses 14-15. Peter's mother-in-law is sick, and Jesus touches her. He's touching a woman who has a fever. You've got two impurities going on here—a woman and a fever.

Go to the next section, verse 28. This is the unclean trifecta. I mean this one takes the cake. Jesus goes from clean land to unclean land. And on unclean land He goes to an unclean place, among the tombs where dead people are—unclean, unclean, unclean. So you have an unclean place. And there He meets unclean people—two guys who are demon-oppressed. And in the midst of this you have unclean pigs. Here's your unclean trifecta—unclean place, unclean person, unclean pigs. The morality of this makes Pharisees shiver. There are cooties all over this story. And the purity patrol knows it.

Well it doesn't stop there. In chapter 9, verses 2-8, Jesus forgives the sins of a paralyzed man and then heals him. He's unclean. In verse 9, Jesus calls Matthew, a tax collector—an unclean occupation—to be His follower. A little later, verse 10, He goes and sits at dinner with tax collectors and sinners—an unclean association.

Down in verse 18, *finally* He's dealing with someone clean. A synagogue leader comes to Jesus and says, "My daughter has just died" (NRSV). This is finally in bounds. This is OK! Jesus can go to the home of a person this pure, this clean. But on the way to her home, what happens? A woman who's been bleeding for years comes up and touches His coat. And He stops and tends to her—the dirty one, the unclean one, the impure one, while the daughter of the clean man lies dead back at home. Ahh, no way.

And then in verse 27, He reaches out and touches the eyes of two blind men. In verse 32, there's a demoniac who is mute.

We've had story after story, after story, after story. You see what's common about this. Here is Jesus, violating every purity law imaginable in His day. I mean, when you begin to think about a Jew looking at this, he is shrinking back. The purity patrol feels like Detective Adrian Monk on a garbage heap.

And what they think about Jesus is very simple—He has dirty hands. He's touching lepers and tax collectors and bleeding women. And He's over there in that country with pigs and demons. Jesus has unclean hands!

But of course that was way back then, and we don't have purity patrols now.

Uncle Harley and Aunt Emma Jean always sat at the back on the right-hand side of the sanctuary at the First Church of the Nazarene in the town where I grew up. They rarely missed a Sunday, but they always sat at the back. During revivals sometimes when the evangelist was making sure we had a long altar call and we were singing about the 17th verse of "Tell Mother I'll Be There in Answer to Her Prayers," somebody would go back to where Uncle Harley was and they'd put their arm around him and say, "Harley, don't you wanna come pray?" And being a teenager, I sat near the back and I could hear his very kind and consistent response, "Thank you for your concern but everything's all right between me and God." And I watched him live; this was my uncle. As far as I could tell, it was. But during World War II, Uncle Harley had picked up the habit of smoking. He had tried—I'd watched him so many times—he'd tried all during his adult life to get rid of that habit, to just kick it. But he just was never able to—always wanted to—but was never quite able to kick the habit. His daughter Debbie, my cousin, died of cancer when she was 12 years old. And a lot of folk around town kind of whispered that it was Uncle Harley's cigarette smoke that killed his daughter. And I'm sure he heard those whispers. His habit earned him a label. And I think that's probably why he sat way in the back every Sunday.

Uncle Harley and Aunt Emma lived two blocks from the Illinois Central Railroad. Macomb was a major stopping point—a place where they checked the engines and did a lot of repair work, so the trains always stopped there. This was the train that went from New Orleans to Chicago. Before the trains would pull into the inspection station in Macomb, all the hobos would get off. They'd have to get off the trains. Uncle Harley and Aunt Emma Jean fed hobos. They fed hobos. Hobos would make marks on curbs and streets that would show other hobos how to find their way to a house where you could get food. I watched this hundreds of times as a little kid playing in their yard.

A hobo would walk up to the door and knock lightly. And he would re-move his hat, and his eyes would go down to his feet. And when the door would open, he would say, "Could you spare a meal, sir? Could you spare a meal, ma'am?" And he would hear, "Yeah. Have a seat right there on the front steps." And he would sit on the front steps and lean against the brick column that was there. Uncle Harley or Aunt Emma Jean would go back in the kitchen where they always kept leftovers and plenty of food, and they would fix him a plate, pour him a tall glass of iced tea, and take it out on the front porch and hand it to him. He would sit there and eat the whole meal. And when he was done, he'd take the empty glass and the empty plate and then tap lightly on the door, hand it back through the screen again, and say, "Thank you. Thank you very much."

I watched this thing happen over and over again. I wish Uncle Harley were alive today. I'd really like to ask him how it felt to be labeled impure. I'd like to ask him why he sat way back in the back. But I'd really like to ask him why he fed the hobos. I'd really like to know that. And I'd love to talk with him about Matt. 23 and 25. Interesting things happen in these two chapters.

In Matt. 23, Jesus is taking on the purity patrol—He's just taking them on. And we find a list that reminds us of the Beatitudes here. There are seven beatitudes and seven "anti-beatitudes." Where the Matt. 5 Beatitudes say "blessed are," the Matt. 23 anti-Beatitudes say "cursed are." And Jesus is saying, "Woe to you scribes and Pharisees, hypocrites!" (vv. 13, 15, 23, 25, 27, 29, NRSV). He's just letting them have it. I find it quite interesting that number six in the Beatitudes is, "Blessed are the pure in heart, for they will see God" (Matt. 5:8), and number five in the anti-Beatitudes is, "Woe to you, scribes and Pharisees, hypocrites! For you clean the outside of the cup and of the plate, but inside they are full of greed and self-indulgence. You blind Pharisee! First clean the inside of the cup, so that the outside also may become clean" (23:25-26, NRSV). "First clean the inside of the cup, so that the outside also may become clean." Can I admit to you that I don't fully understand what that means? But one thing I do think it means is that you cannot look at what is external about people and be dead sure that you're reading what is internal about people. You really can't know that for sure, because there are a lot of folks whose label may well say pure. The purity patrol has stickered them. They're fine. And yet, there is something missing and something lacking that is critically important. "Blessed are the pure in heart, for they will see God."

I'd also want Uncle Harley to tell me about Matt. 25. I think Matthew writes these Beatitudes way back in chapter 5 and then explains them all the way through the Gospel. And here in Matt. 25:31, I find an interesting thing: "When the Son of Man comes in his glory, and all the angels with him, then he will sit on the throne of his glory" (NRSV). Just as He sat down to teach on the mount, He now sits on His throne to reign. Here is Jesus—He has now come and He is bringing the reign and rule of God to bear everywhere—I mean *everywhere*. And here He is—He sits down and He divides people into the sheep on His right hand and the goats at His left hand, and He begins to talk to each group about what they've done. You know this text, verse 34: "The king will say to those at his right hand, 'Come, you that are blessed [there's that Beatitude word again] by my Father, inherit the kingdom prepared for you from the foundation of the world." Why? "'I was hungry and you gave me food, I was thirsty and you gave me something to drink, I was a stranger and you welcomed me, I was naked and you gave me clothing, I was sick and you took care of me, I was in prison and you visited me.' Then the righteous will answer him, [pay close attention, friends] 'Lord, when was it that we saw you ["Blessed are the pure in heart, for they will see God."] hungry and gave you food, or thirsty and gave you something to drink? And when was it that we saw you a stranger and welcomed you, or naked and gave you clothing? And when was it that we saw you sick or in prison and visited you?' And the king will answer them, 'Truly, I tell you, just as you did it to one of the least of these who are members of my family, you did it to me'" (vv. 35-40, NRSV).

Whoa! Here are these people, these sheep at the right hand at the Day of Judgment, and Jesus is here saying,

> "Blessings upon you; the Kingdom is for such as you. Come and inherit all that has been provided for you" (see v. 34).

And what did they do to receive such blessing? They got their hands dirty. They went around touching unclean people in the world, not knowing that in these people they were seeing God.

> "When did we see You?"

> "I was in the ones who are needy."

But to the ones on His left hand—the goats—you see what He says to them?

> "He will say to those at his left, 'You that are accursed [the anti-beatitude word], depart from me into the eternal fire prepared for the devil and his angels; for I was hungry and you gave me no food, I was thirsty and you gave me nothing to drink, I was a stranger and you did not

welcome me, naked and you did not give me clothing, sick and in prison and you did not visit me.' Then they will also answer, 'Lord, when was it that we saw you hungry or thirsty or a stranger or naked or sick or in prison, and did not take care of you?' Then he will answer them, 'Truly I tell you, just as you did not do it to one of the least of these, you did not do it to me.' And these will go away into eternal punishment, but the righteous into eternal life" (vv. 41-46, NRSV).

Who are these folk? They saw unclean people in the world, and they kept their hands clean. "I'm not going to touch them. If I touch them, the purity patrol might label me. I'm not touching them!"

I was raised a Nazarene. There are five generations of us now. Purity of heart has been our language for years and years. But sometimes when I look at us Nazarenes, it seems to me that our hands are too clean to be the followers of Jesus. We look at our hands, and we are unbothered by the need of the world. We are the religious elite, and we don't touch those kinds of people. We gather in our sanctuaries and talk about them, but we don't ever touch them.

I wonder if when Jesus says, "Blessed are the pure in heart" (5:8, NRSV) —I wonder if He's saying that to them because their hands are dirty— dirty like the hands of Jesus?

I was imagining when I got up this morning about the day the Son of Man will return—sheep on the right, goats on the left, with a *big* banquet for all the sheep—a *big* banquet. I think I saw something. I think I saw Uncle Harley sitting at a table, fully delivered from his nicotine habit. And I saw him surrounded by a bunch of hobos. And for the life of me, they all looked like Jesus.

"Blessed are the pure in heart," who know how to get their hands dirty as Jesus got His hands dirty. In the next person we serve, we may be seeing God. We may be seeing God.

Let's pray:
> *Gracious God, we proudly wear the label "Holiness people" in this world. May we not wear that label without understanding what our hands are supposed to be doing. And may purity cause us to go where Jesus goes and do what Jesus does, until that day when He separates us to His right and says, "You were always blessed. You took care of your fellow creatures." Grant us the purity of heart to have dirty hands. In the name of the Christ, we come and we go. And all God's people said, "Amen."*

3
GOD'S IMAGERS:
HOLINESS THROUGH
THE PAGES OF THE BIBLE
SCOTT DANIELS

introduction and interview

Scott grew up in a family full of preachers—his dad, both grandfathers, and all his uncles were Holiness preachers. He says that as a young person he looked for anything else he could do but preach. However, the call of God that changed and directed his life came in his high school years during a World Youth Congress. He gave up an interest in journalism for the study of religion at Northwest Nazarene University in Nampa, Idaho, where he graduated in 1988.

After a brief ministry assignment in Seattle, he moved to Pasadena, California, and continued in ministry to teens and college students while completing a Ph.D. in theological ethics from Fuller Theological Seminary. After teaching three years at Azusa Pacific University and then seven years at Southern Nazarene University in Bethany, Oklahoma, he pastored the Richardson Church of the Nazarene (RCN) near Dallas. In 2006 he accepted the position of senior pastor at Pasadena First Church of the Nazarene.

I asked him about moving from academic studies and teaching to pastoral ministry. He said,

I always believed that God had called me to preach. I firmly believe that the church is the local church. Even when I was teaching, I made a conscious decision to be part of a pastoral staff. I treasure my years in education because they were years God used to shape me theologically and biblically.

How did you develop as a Holiness preacher?

While I was in seminary in Pasadena, I was also on staff with Steve Green. Through a combination of study, Steve's preaching, and our synergetic friendship, different pieces of the Scriptures began to fit together for me like never before, and I began to realize that we have a really great theological tradition. My ethics studies also got me really interested in John Wesley. The study of Wesley helped me realize that holiness is not just a doctrine but also a method. During that time holiness stopped being for me simply the repetition of key phrases that I learned growing up and became much more a way of understanding God's intentions for how He wants His people to make a difference in the world.

In what way do you define "holiness" in this sermon as a relational distinctive?

I certainly believe there is a ceremonial aspect of holiness—the idea of being uniquely set apart. Israel was set apart from all the other nations, and the early believers in Christ were called out from the world. The aspect of holiness I failed to understand as a young person was the relational dimension. I think my parents came through the church during a time when the ceremonial aspect of holiness was emphasized so heavily that the people who claimed holiness were folks who had so separated themselves from the culture that they had become little help to the world, and few people were attracted to their lives. The "aha" for me was when I came to understand that God's call upon people to be separate—like His call to Abraham —is always for the sake of becoming a blessing and an instrument of God's grace and love in the world. I understood what we were called from; *it was realizing what we are called* to *that I was missing.*

Why did you begin your series of Holiness sermons in the "Hymn of Creation"—as you refer to it—in Genesis?

Genesis makes it so clear that God created us for relationship with Him, and as a reflection of His image, for relationship with others and with the creation. I love to study and preach from the first 11 chapters of Genesis because they so insightfully describe the world as fragmented, broken, and violent. When the reader comes to the end of chapter 11, he or she realizes that God's mission in the world has to be the restoration of His marred image in us.

What was the result of this concentration on Holiness preaching?

The Holiness series was the first series I preached when I got to RCN. I wanted my first words to this congregation to be a clear articulation of who I believe we are as a Holiness people. I used several different places—or traditions—in Scripture (Genesis, the Deutero-Historic books, Wisdom Literature, the Prophets, the Gospels, the Epistles, and even Revelation) to demonstrate that holiness is a key idea throughout the Bible. I wanted the people at RCN to recognize that the theme of holiness is not just the product of two or three proof texts that we pull out and use to maintain some arbitrary denominational distinctive. I wanted them to see the many facets of holiness throughout the Scripture. I was overwhelmed by their response. Although some of what I had to say was familiar for longtime Holi-

ness folks, a great deal of the series—especially the relational aspect of holiness—
was a different way of looking at holiness and a different language for talking
about holiness than a lot of the old-time Nazarene folks had grown up hearing.
Rather than reacting negatively, however, they continue to be excited about how
the life of holiness is coming alive for them. For new believers it just seems like the
natural way of understanding our relationship to God. I never feel as if I have to
sell new Christians a party line; they more often than not commit to the holy life
because they understand that God has called them to be holy as He is holy. And
how is He holy? Relationally. He loves us. So we should love each other.

sermon: "god's imagers: holiness through the pages of the bible"

I would like to begin a journey with you today that I am calling "Holiness Through the Pages of the Bible." Part of the reason I want to do that is I want to let you know what I believe to be most true about God and about who we are to be as His people in the world, but I also want to talk to us about a very important aspect of who we are as a church and as a particular tradition within the Christian Church.

When Debbie and I lived in California, several years ago now, I was the university pastor at Pasadena First Church, and we had several new Christians who were part of our university group.

Most of our college kids were just starting to figure out who Jesus was, so they had little concern for what it meant to be a Nazarene. We had a group there at Paz Naz that worked diligently to support pro-life issues, and they called themselves Nazarenes for Life.

I'll never forget when one of our new Christians—a wonderful young woman by the name of Lisa—brought me the worship folder from church one Sunday. She was very distressed. In the worship folder there was an advertisement for a group that was meeting after church on Sunday night and the ad read, "You are invited! Anyone interested in participating in Nazarenes for Life, there is an important meeting tonight at 7:30."

Lisa was so flabbergasted. She wanted to know, "What kind of person would pledge to be a Nazarene *for life!*" Apparently she thought the church was having a secret meeting afterward for all those who were pledging to remain Nazarenes for life. Lisa liked the church well enough, but forcing her to commit until "death do us part" seemed a little much.

Well, I hope that you like being a part of a Church of the Nazarene, but I hope that your first commitment is to Jesus Christ. But I want to talk to us just a little bit about what it means to be committed to this idea of "holiness"—which is really the idea that formed the Church of the Nazarene and other churches that are part of the Holiness tradition.

I'm convinced that there is a lot of confusion about what it means to even seek after holiness. In fact, there are at least three distorted views.

One of the distorted views is the idea that holiness is really about our individual ability to make a complete commitment to Christ. So, if I want to be holy, what I really need to do is commit, commit, and commit some more. Although commitment certainly is a key aspect to the holy life, being holy is not just making one more commitment.

Some of us were raised that way because we were raised going to camp, right? So we can remember "all the times and places where God reached us with His graces." Right? Because we went to summer camp and we made one more commitment and oftentimes when we preach in our churches, we preach, "If there's something that you have deep down inside that you have not committed, then come and commit it," we come to believe that our relationship with Christ is dependent upon our strength and ability to make and keep our commitments to Him.

Therefore at some point we should have committed enough that we have nothing left to commit, and at that point we must have become holy. The distortion and problem with this idea is that we can come to believe that being what God wants us to be depends upon us gritting our teeth, pulling ourselves up by our bootstraps, and saying, "All right, I *will* become what God wants me to become! And this time I really mean it!" To believe that we can become holy through our own power completely underestimates the depth of God's holiness. If we are to become holy as He is holy, it is going to take much more than just our decision to be holy.

Some of us who were raised in the church, especially the Church of the Nazarene and other traditions like it, came to believe that what holiness looks like is legalism—a deep, rich, sometimes ugly form of legalism. Holiness as legalism is the second distorted view. For the legalist, what it means to be holy is to exclude everything unholy from the circle of our life—to cut ourselves off from everything that might even remotely look secular.

If that's the case, if what holiness is about is a form of legalism, then the Pharisees were the most godly people in the Scriptures, for they were convinced that the reason the Kingdom had not yet come was because the people had not kept God's Law carefully enough.

The reason they excluded tax collectors, sinners, and even the sick from fellowship—and the reason they crucified Jesus—was because they believed that God wanted them to purify their life by casting out any part of their community that was unholy. And yet in the Gospels we discover that Jesus is constantly doing battle with those who are the very best at being legalistic. In an amazing irony, those who were trying to be most holy through obedience to the Law were demonstrated as being the most unholy.

Speaking vulnerably, having grown up as a fourth generation Nazarene—third generation ordained elder—if holiness is the legalism that some of the people I knew growing up with had in their lives, the legalism that made them bitter, angry people whose children despised them and their religion and whose congregations feared them, I don't really want anything to do with it. We shouldn't be surprised that most of the people who knew those legalists didn't want anything to do with that form of holiness either.

Think about it. Have you ever known a legalist who was winning people to Christ? Most people who see that kind of life want no part of it, not because it is too hard, but because the spirit of the legalist is so unattractive to them.

So, holiness is not a hyper form of legalism.

We've abandoned that a little bit, and I think we have picked up a third distorted view, which is the idea that holiness is some kind of emotionalism. From this perspective, to be holy is to have a kind of emotionalism that is constantly a part of our lives—what my friends and I call "holy goose bumps."

For those that equate holiness with the emotionalism of the faith, to be holy is to pursue forms of worship or to pursue our relationship with God in such a way that we finally get some holy goose bumps and once we've had that, then we know that our lives are made holy.

Please don't misunderstand me this morning. I hope that as we gather to worship, there are a whole lot of holy-goose-bump moments in our lives together. But you know what? There will be some times when there aren't those holy goose bumps, and that doesn't mean that we're any less holy because those goose bumps aren't always there.

Let me use marriage as a comparison. There have been frequent moments in our years of marriage when the fires of passion for one another burns hot. There are hopefully wonderful moments of romance in all of our marriage relationships. But all of us who have been married longer than six weeks know that much of marriage is making dinner, washing dishes, working in the yard, paying bills, and figuring out what to do with the kids.

Yet all of us know we are just as married—if not more so—when we are picking weeds together or even arguing with each other as we are when we are making goo-goo eyes at each other on Valentine's Day.

In the same way we are just as holy—maybe even more so—when we are wrestling with God and with the difficult stuff of life as we are when we feel ecstatic emotions of the faith that come and go.

Moving past our distortions—and I'm sure we could think of several more—there are two important convictions I want to share at the beginning. These are two very deep convictions I have about the idea of holiness. In this series I am going to emphasize these convictions over and over again until we get them.

The first thing I believe deeply is this—holiness is biblical. In fact, that's why we are going to take these three months to go through the Scriptures and hear what they have to say about the holy life. Please understand this, if holiness is something the Nazarenes came up with, then we need to abandon it. If holiness is even something the father of this particular theological tradition—a man by the name of John Wesley who was an Anglican minister in the 18th century—came up with and we have been holding on to it for 200-plus years now, we need to get rid of it.

But I believe holiness is not some kind of an add-on a small denomi-

nation like ours came up with so we would have something that
makes us unique. I believe in the idea of holiness because I believe it is
thoroughly biblical. As we look through these various biblical texts,
we will see that God's call upon His people from Abraham to the Early Church is that we become a holy people. We are to be holy as he is
holy. Holiness is biblical.

It is the second conviction that I want to focus on this morning, and that
conviction is this—holiness is relational. The key to understanding what
the holy life is all about is to understand that the fundamental aspect of
holiness is its relational aspect.

One of my favorite quotes from John Wesley is this: There is "no holiness
but social holiness" (preface to *Hymns and Sacred Poems*). What Wesley
meant when he said that is this—the central aspect of the holy life is
found in our relationships. Holiness can only be lived out in relationship
to God and to one another. There's no such thing as holiness or a holy
life that excludes our relationship with others. All holiness finds itself
lived out in the social areas of our lives.

That is why I want us to begin this series with Gen. 1:26-27. I am convinced that in these verses we discover the root or the key to what God
wants us to be and to do in our lives. Let's look at it together again.

> "Then God said, 'Let us make humankind in our image, according to
> our likeness; and let them have dominion over the fish of the sea, and
> over the birds of the air, and over the cattle, and over all the wild ani-
> mals of the earth, and over every creeping thing that creeps upon the
> earth.'
>
> "So God created humankind in his image,
>   in the image of God he created them;
>   male and female he created them" (NRSV).

One of the things theologians have wrestled with again and again is the
question, What does it mean for the text to say we were created in the image of God? What does it mean for us to be in the image of God?

> Some people have tried to describe the image of God in human per-
> sons as rationality. In this view, the way we are most like God can be
> found in the way we are not like the rest of creation. So, some scholars
> have reasoned, if we look at humans and we compare them to the rest
> of creation, one of the things we find in human persons is a higher

form of rationality and all kinds of implications that follow from that. Only humans, for example, tell stories. Only humans can reflect upon and give meaning to their memories.

Although I certainly agree that our rationality is part of what makes us unique as human persons, I don't think any one quality can be viewed as the sum of what it means to be in God's image. The problem is that if any one quality becomes the sum of what it means to be in God's image, then those who have that quality in abundance could be considered more in God's image than others who lack it.

> For example, if rationality is what causes us to be in God's image, then Albert Einstein is more in the image of God than a person who is mentally handicapped or challenged. I have a feeling someone who has worked closely with God's special and challenged folks— someone like Henri Nouwen—would want to dispute that idea.
>
>> In one of the churches I have been a part of, there was a mentally handicapped young man named Nathan who every Sunday would pray the simplest but most sincere prayer for the worship team before the service began. Each week I would be moved to tears by the honest, vulnerable childlikeness of his prayers. Certainly we would never want to say that somehow the physicist had more of God's image than Nathan.
>
> Sometimes theologians have argued that we are like God or in the image of God because we have an eternal nature about us—a soul. Although I believe our eternal standing with God may be part of what it means to be in His image, I believe the text gives us a much richer insight into the uniqueness of humanness than simply our eternality.

To really understand what I think it means to be in the image of God, we have to understand a little bit of the context of Genesis. I want to show you just a couple of verses in Genesis 1. Look with me, if you will, back a little bit in the text to Gen. 1:16. We are going to look at this text in more detail next week, but I want you to notice in the great "Hymn of Creation" how, in day four, the sun and the moon are described.

"God made the two great lights—the greater light to rule the day and the lesser light to rule the night—and the stars" (NRSV).

Look also with me at verse 21. On the fifth day God is creating all the fish and all the birds, and in verse 21 it says,

"So God created the great sea monsters and every living creature that moves, of every kind, with which the waters swarm, and every winged bird of every kind. And God saw that it was good" (NRSV).

I point out those two texts because of the really interesting language the text uses to describe the role of the sun and moon as God places them in the dome of the sky. The text says that God created the sun to rule the day and the moon to rule the night (and the stars). I agree with some Old Testament scholars who believe that the reason the scripture describes the sun and moon as "rulers" of day and night is because the cultures that surrounded Israel—cultures like Babylon, Assyria, and even Egypt—in one form or another worshiped the sun and the moon. The first readers of Genesis would already understand that the sun and moon are not just two unique orbs in the dome of the sky but rulers of the day and night and are worshiped as such by all of the surrounding nations. The sun and moon are two great gods, two great rulers.

Therefore the opening hymn of Genesis is saying something very theologically radical and important to these early people. The hymn declares that Israel's God created the sun to rule the day and the moon to rule the night, but the Israelites don't worship them as the greatest of all gods, because their God created them. God's people don't worship the sun and the moon, because they are somebody else's inferior gods.

Again verse 21 describes God creating "the great sea monsters" of the deep. The term there in Hebrew is an interesting word. The word used is *tiamat*. The word *tiamat* is difficult for us to translate not only into English but also into our culture. Most of our translations use "sea monsters," which can make us think of huge sea creatures. Often in children's church, in the felt-board version of creation, we will put up a whale to depict the great sea monsters of the deep.

The only problem with this is that there wasn't a whole lot of whale watching taking place in ancient Israel. So many OT scholars would argue that the great sea monsters of the deep are not whales or really large fish, but the large creatures of the waters surrounding the Semitic cultures that also took on godlike status. Some scholars think they are probably referring here to the crocodiles or the alligators of the Nile; for river-dwelling cultures these would be the great sea monsters that they would fear and that would shape their lives. Another reason for proposing this interpretation is that it is interesting that once again cultures like the Babylonians, Egyptians, and others worshiped gods like the crocodile, the great sea monsters of the deep.

If I had more time this morning I would point to several other places in the first three chapters of Genesis where there are likely references to idolatry. One more example is the serpent in the Garden of Eden that lures Eve into tasting the forbidden fruit.

If you ever watch old biblical movies like *The Ten Commandments,* you will notice that Pharaoh almost always has the same creature on his head—a snake. The snake—a critical god of fertility for ancient cultures—became the symbol Pharaoh used to demonstrate that he had the power over life and death.

The point I want you to get is this: the creation narratives of Genesis are filled with references to gods—or more properly—to images of gods.

So what does this have to do with humankind and our being created in God's image?

Let me give you a hint. Most of you probably will remember that the second of the Ten Commandments is, "You shall not make for yourselves any graven image" (see Exod. 20:4, KJV).

Have you ever stopped to ponder why God gets so upset at the making of graven images? What if the people made images of Yahweh simply to remind them that He is present? What is so wrong with that? Does God have an image problem? Is God like me, does He just not like to see pictures of himself? We all hate pictures of ourselves. None of us in this room has ever looked at a picture of himself or herself and said, "Oh, that's so me! I look just like that. I love my hair!" All of us look at pictures and say, "I don't look like that. Everybody else in the world is photogenic, but not me."

God's problem is not vanity. God does not look at images or idols or pictures of himself and say, "No. That's not Me. I don't look like that. My nose isn't that big!"

The first chapter of Genesis is saying something really profound, theologically, to us—and that is this—God has not created images of himself, nor does He want us fashioning images of himself, because He has created us in His image. "In the image of God he created them; male and female he created them" (v. 27, NRSV). This means that uniquely in all of creation you and I are created to be the image or reflection of God in the world.

That is why we have been given all these amazing human gifts: gifts of rationality, storytelling, memory, even our gifts of eternality—all of those things that are part of being human. We have those gifts because we are uniquely called to be God's reflection and image in the world.

In order to understand holiness, we have this idea first—we were created to be God's image and reflection in the world.

As the narratives of Gen. 2 and 3 progress through the story of the Fall, we see an interesting dynamic unfold in the relationship between God, humankind, and three other parties—self, creation, and others.

What I would like you to do in your mind is think of two stick people in the middle of a page and then in your mind draw several little arrows: one between God and humankind (the two figures), another between the two figures, a third from the persons pointing down to creation, and the last a curved arrow that goes from the persons back toward themselves.

The first arrow acknowledges the primary relationship of life between God and human beings. In the early part of the Eden narrative, God and humankind walk openly in relationship to each other. God shows up each day and walks in the cool of the garden with Adam and Eve. This is a wonderful image. God shows up and says, "Hey, it's time for our walk. Let's go." And they walk together, God and His creation talking and chatting in a wonderful, peaceful, and unbroken relationship with each other.

As the humans are in this unbroken relationship with God, they also find that they are in an unbroken relationship with each other (the second arrow). This is symbolized in the garden in the way that Adam and Eve live with each other and care for each other in complete vulnerability, equality, and transparency. There is an unbroken mutuality in the relationship between Adam and Eve.

Not only are they in an unbroken relationship with each other as they walk with God, but they are in an unbroken relationship with creation (arrow number three) as well. In the garden, Adam and Eve get to do some interesting things. Adam names the animals. They live in harmony in the midst of the garden. As they live in this kind of unbroken paradise, they care and have a proper dominion—which is the opposite of domination—over the creation, and the creation responds in kind.

But there is also an unbroken relationship (the curved arrow) in the love of self. We discover that Adam and Eve are naked and unashamed of who or what they are. In their nakedness they are able to have mutuality with each other, but they are also able to be open and honest with each other without fear.

Thus, to be in the image of God means that we are created in such a way that as we walk in relationship with God, we have the ability to reflect or "image" the love of God to each other, to the creation, and even in the proper way that we love ourselves. This is the way things are supposed to be. Humankind is supposed to walk in an unbroken relationship of trust with God, which opens us up to an unbroken relationship with each other, which spills over into a proper dominion and care for the creation and culminates in the proper valuing of our unique personhood as individuals.

But then the Fall happens. Eve and Adam partake of the fruit, and as soon as they partake of this fruit, the most amazing but tragic thing happens. The relationship with God is immediately broken. When God shows up to walk with them, what do Adam and Eve do? They jump in the bushes and hide. They hide so well that God cannot find them. God comes and looks for them and calls out to them and cries, "Adam, where are you, where are you?" The relationship is broken and shattered. (Take your pen and draw an X through the arrow that links the relationship between humankind and God.)

And as soon as that relationship with God is broken, guess what, everything else is broken too. When God finds Adam—and this is one of my favorite parts of the Genesis story—God says, "Adam, what have you done?" Adam responds with a double dose of blame. "Don't look at me; this *woman* that *You* created." He is blaming everybody except himself. It is her fault for luring me, and it is Your fault, God, for making her in the first place. Adam's blame breaks the relationship between himself and Eve. (So draw an X over the arrow depicting the relationship with each other.) Later we will see that this brokenness between people escalates in a hurry and Cain will kill his brother Abel.

Who or what does Eve blame? She blames the serpent. She points her finger at creation. "Don't look at me," says Eve. "Creation lured me into a love for it." And we see out of this brokenness resulting from the Fall comes the misuse of creation that puts the humans at odds with the garden. (So now put an X between humans and creation.)

We even find in the text the brokenness of self. The human creatures suddenly discover they are naked and ashamed, and they begin to cover themselves and hide from one another. (Place a final X on the arrow representing proper love of self.)

So here is the point I want to make with you today. The problem we find ourselves in is fundamentally this—our relationship with God is broken, and because our relationship with God is broken, so are all the other relationships of our lives.

Because the relationship with God is broken, the relationship with my children is broken; the relationship with my wife is broken; the relationships with my friends, with my community, and most especially with my enemies are broken.

The proper relationship of humans with creation is broken. We don't care for creation as we ought to. And the relationship with myself is broken. I find myself way too insecure at times and way too proud at others. The world is one big violent, angry, abusive, relational mess!

But if you get nothing else out of these next several weeks on holiness, I want you to remember this. There is no holiness except social holiness. You see what Wesley and other Holiness folks understood is that just as our broken relationship with God leads to broken relationships with others, the creation, and the self, the restoration of our relationship with God through His grace and love ought to lead to the restoration of our relationships with others, the creation, and the self.

To be holy is to participate in the restoration of the proper image of God in us. As we are in renewed relationship with God, we are transformed more and more into the likeness of His nature and character of love.

Through His transforming grace, the love God has given to us becomes reflected to others, to creation, and to the self. In this way we become God's imagers.

Here is the key to what we Holiness folks believe. We are convinced that God's grace is meant not just to forgive us but also to transform us into the original image of Him that He created us to be.

And where do we see that image most clearly? Most profoundly we see that image in the life of Jesus Christ, and that is why we say again and again that we are to be like Jesus. What God wants to do in our lives is to shape, to mold, and to form us into the very image and likeness of His Son, who was the ultimate image of God the Father.

And so my question for us this morning is not just a holiness question but *the* holiness question. How are the relationships in your life today?

How is the relationship with your children?

How is the relationship between you and your spouse?

How are the relationships between you and your colleagues at work?

How are the relationships with your neighbors?

How are the relationships even with your enemies?

It is because holiness is at its core relational that Jesus can say, "If you are ever at the altar (committing yourself one more time at camp) and you realize that your brother or sister has something against you, get up and leave and be reconciled to your brother or sister and then come back to the altar" (see Matt. 5:23-24).

Holiness is not so much about what we can give to God so He can go, "Oh, you are such a holy people! I have never had a sacrifice quite like that before."

But if you are at the altar, and you realize your brother or sister has something against you, leave it, because holy people recognize that the place of holiness is in the relationships of our lives.

That is why Jesus says things like this: "You have heard that it was said, 'An eye for an eye and a tooth for a tooth.' But I say to you, Do not resist an evildoer. But if anyone strikes you on the right cheek, turn the other also; . . . and if anyone forces you to go one mile, go also the second mile'" (see vv. 38-41, NRSV). For in this Kingdom, we don't just love those who love us, but like the Heavenly Father, we love our enemies as well as our friends.

This is why John can tell us that those who love are born of God and know God (see 1 John 4:7). Do you want to know if you are God's holy people? You will only know it if you love one another.

Some of the most committed, legalistic, and holy-goose-bumped people I have known in my life have also been some of the most critical, harsh, and unloving. If you give everything you have to God, but have not love, you are nothing.

If you don't drink, dance, smoke, or chew, or go with girls that do, and have not love, you are nothing but a creepy conservative. If you run aisles, jump pews, and sing with both hands in the air, but don't have love, you are nothing but an embarrassment to your children. How sad that we have too often pursued the holy life and missed its essential ingredient—love.

God wants us to be a holy people. And God is not going to stop with us until He forms us into the image He created us to be. So my questions for us today as His Church are

How are our relationships?

When people come to this church and people come to know that you are a believer, what kind of God do they see reflected in the relationships of your life?

Do they see the God who is reflected in the life of Jesus? For if they don't, then He is not through with you or me yet, for holiness is what He longs for in our lives.

And there is no holiness but social holiness.

4

BLUE JEANS &
TENNIS SHOES
ROGER HAHN

introduction and interview

In this camp meeting message, "Blue Jeans and Tennis Shoes," Dr. Roger Hahn, dean of the faculty at Nazarene Theological Seminary, presents the Holiness message in down-to-earth language and images. In addition to his academic work, he is a frequent camp meeting speaker as well as the leader and regular preacher at the liturgical service at Kansas City First Church of the Nazarene.

He remembers that when he was five, an evangelist in his home church predicted he would become a preacher. He lived with that expectation until he was called to the ministry during his freshman year at Southern Nazarene University (SNU). From there he went to Nazarene Theological Seminary and upon graduation became pastor of the First Church of the Nazarene, Durham, North Carolina, near Duke University where he completed doctoral New Testament studies. Following this, he taught New Testament at SNU for 15 years and since 1994 has served as professor of New Testament at NTS, becoming dean of the faculty in 2002.

I asked him about the response of people—in classrooms as well as camp meetings.

Your metaphor of "Blue Jeans and Tennis Shoes" is intended to connect with people. You suggest that the Holiness message has not been applicable or credible in some way.

I think sometimes this happens, and I don't feel I've been the victim of that very much, but I hear people who say they are.

In this sermon at a camp meeting, how did the people receive the Holiness message?

People at camp meetings are expecting Holiness messages. People receive it to some degree in the way it's delivered. I've tried to deliver it with a sense of grace and hope and invitation; I've tried to create a sense of aspiration and desire. People respond very well to that. One of the things I learned in seminary in my Wesley class from Greathouse was that Wesley said, "I preach holiness drawingly." And I always tried to do that. There used to be some folks who preached it in a way that was not attractive—they put people off because it was so harsh. I wouldn't be surprised at resistance there.

How would people who listen to this message describe holiness in their own lives?

I think there would be a variety of responses because of a variety of orientations they bring to the question of what holiness is. I'm reasonably sure that for some it's a bunch of dos and don'ts. But there are a large number of people who I think would describe it as Christlikeness, having relationship with Christ, a wholehearted, full commitment to Christ—that kind of thing.

Do they understand the distinction between the initial work and the work of entire sanctification?

Some do. Certainly folks who have experience in our tradition do. My experience with folks who are new to the tradition is that they wonder how this is different from what would just happen naturally if you just kept obeying God.

What is your response?

I say, if you just keep obeying God, this will happen naturally, because I believe that God will bring you to this moment, and the degree of crisis you experience may depend partly on your personality—on what's happening in your life and all kinds of things. There'll be a point when you make a transition from being a Christian in your own strength to being a Christian in God's strength, from trying to manage all this yourself, from yourself being in control to God being in control. There'll be a time that you ultimately relinquish total Lordship to Jesus.

Do you think that Nazarenes see themselves as Holiness people?

I'm afraid the answer nowadays is probably no. I'm sure there are great numbers who do—there are congregations that do. And maybe it's because I'm in a large metropolitan area with a church full of folks who've come into the church in recent years and don't often use that term to describe themselves.

What, then, is the future of the Holiness community?

It depends on what we do and how we respond—those of us who care about it. I don't think we want to obsess over it, because preserving our identity just to preserve our identity is idolatry. God has given us something we think is very important, and we need to be more intentional and more focused on transmitting this heritage. I see signs that the church in a variety of ways is trying to do that—such as the church I'm a part of with a Sunday night series on holiness. Because of that desire, we don't want to lose that focus on this very important message.

On campus—how much awareness is there among the faculty and students about being in the Holiness tradition?

Quite frankly, I think the greatest awareness of it anywhere in the denomination is among the faculty. That's been my experience—both when I was at SNU and now at NTS. The faculty members talk about this issue and ponder and work on ways we can constructively contribute to perpetuate our message and our identity more than I hear anywhere else in the church. On the other hand, I think if you did a random poll of our students, there are a higher percentage of them than folks in our local churches who would call themselves Holiness people. But we haven't won this battle yet among students either. They understand there's something there, but some of them are still trying to figure out what it is—in part because they get a different message at church than they get at seminary.

How should the Holiness message be presented to attract newcomers in the pew as well as students?

I think it should be presented as Christlikeness. That's primarily because that's the way the Bible most frequently paints it. The central figure of the Christian faith is Jesus. We become Christlike not just through our effort but through a divine infusion of grace, without which this can't happen. I think that's clear in the New Testament.

I do have a great deal of optimism for the message of holiness and am confident that if our church doesn't carry the ball, someone else will. This message has not died in 2,000 years; it can't die because it's right out of the heart of the New Testament—right out of the heart of God.

sermon: "blue jeans and tennis shoes"

Second Cor. 3:1-18 will be the text for this evening's message.

"Are we beginning to recommend ourselves again? Or as some, we don't need letters of recommendation to you or from you, do we? You are our letter written on our hearts, read and recognized by everyone; for you are making it clear that you are a letter of Christ served by us, written not with ink but by the Spirit of the living God, not on tablets of stone but on tablets of human hearts.

"And we have such confidence through Christ toward God. Not that we are sufficient from ourselves to consider anything as deriving from our very selves, but our sufficiency derives from God, who has made us sufficient to be ministers of a new covenant, a covenant not of the letter but of the Spirit, for the letter kills, and the Spirit makes alive.

"Now if the ministry of death, in letters engraved in stone, came in glory, so that the sons of Israel were not able to gaze at the face of Moses because of the fading glory of his face, how much more shall not the ministry of the Spirit be in glory? For if there was glory for the ministry of condemnation, how much more the ministry of righteousness will abound in glory? For that which has been glorious is not even glorious now in this regard, because of the surpassing glory. For if that which was fading faded through glory, how much more that which abides forever will abide in glory?

"Therefore, because we have such a hope, we use great confidence—and we are not like Moses, who put a veil over his face in order that the children of Israel might not gaze at the end of that which was fading away. But their minds were hardened. For unto this very day the same veil remains at the reading of the old covenant. It is not uncovered because only in Christ is it taken away. But unto this very day whenever Moses is read, a veil lies over their hearts. But when one turns to the Lord, the veil is removed.

"And the Lord is the Spirit; and freedom is where the Spirit of the Lord is. And we all with an unveiled face, as we are reflecting as in a mirror the glory of the Lord, we are being transformed into the same image from one degree of glory to another degree of glory, just as from the Lord, who is the Spirit" (author's translation).

Let us pray.

Father, speak to our hearts this evening. Help us not to simply hear another sermon and another preacher. Help us to hear Your Spirit speaking to our hearts, making Your Word alive and pertinent to our lives. And grant us grace to walk in the light You shed on our paths. We ask in Christ's name and for His sake. Amen.

If you want a major surprise in your life, get married. It doesn't matter how well you think you know somebody, there's nothing like getting married to him or her to discover you didn't know much about him or her at all.

Dorothy and I had been engaged for over two and a half years before we were married. We had that long engagement partly because our preengagement period was fairly short, partly because we had a certain parent—namely, my mother—to satisfy that this was really a workable situation, and partly because we didn't have any money.

And there were a whole variety of reasons. But one of the reasons was that we were sure we wanted to invest a great deal of quality time in getting to know each other very, very well so that our marriage would be a great success.

We had talked for thousands and thousands of hours, I think. At least we were up really late lots of nights talking and talking and talking. Maybe it's how well we knew each other that was part of our problem—I don't know. Little did Dorothy and I know how prophetic that very first weekend of our married life would be.

Dorothy taught school in Oklahoma City until noon on Friday. Then she got on an airplane and flew to Denver, where I took her keys to the car away from her because she has a very ornery brother who I suspected was up to something nasty.

She flew on down to Colorado Springs, and I drove down to Colorado Springs Saturday morning for the wedding rehearsal at Colorado Springs First Church—along with the car keys. I apparently had also taken her luggage keys. And it was not a happy lady that met me that morning asking if she could borrow the keys to get her toothbrush, thank you!

Well, the rehearsal was Saturday morning, and the wedding was Saturday night. We were in church Sunday morning in Brush, Colorado. She kind of shook the rice out of her corsage, walked in, and said, "Hi. I'm Dorothy Blann, and this is my husband, Roger Hahn." We were off to a great start.

Then we headed to the Monday morning Memorial Day services at the Hamlet, Nebraska, cemetery, where the ancestors of the Hahn family are all buried and are all worshiped every Memorial Day. And then we went back to Bethany to load up and go to Hot Springs, Arkansas, to begin a ministry assignment that Saturday.

One week and 16 hours after our wedding was our first Sunday dinner with our senior pastor that summer. And the next several Sundays we were invited to the homes of various people from that church—Hot Springs First Church, that is. Some of you have been there. It was the old building downtown.

And about a month later we had our very first Sunday dinner

in our own home—by ourselves. But we had talked about it through that week as we realized, nobody else was going to invite us out anymore. And we were going to have Sunday dinner, and what a great occasion it was going to be.

And so I walked into that little apartment—that hot, little apartment in Hot Springs, Arkansas, that Sunday noon. My tie was off and on the chair. My coat was neatly laid on another chair. My shoes were placed neatly spaced down the hall. And in 15 seconds I was coming back through the hall in my blue jeans and tennis shoes.

I was ready to relax and have a comfortable Sunday afternoon with my new wife. But she was still in the living room when I came back in my blue jeans and tennis shoes. And for the first time in our married life I saw "the look."

"Uh, what's wrong?" I asked in my youthful innocence.

"Why are you undressed?" she fumed.

I was stunned. I was dressed. "I've got on my everyday clothes," I said. What could be more obvious? I thought.

"And what's wrong with wearing your Sunday clothes for Sunday dinner?" she asked.

Well, I was relieved to hear that that was the only issue. I knew the answer to that question; I had grown up on a farm. And I had been taught the answer to that question all of my life.

"You can't wear your Sunday clothes at home," I said, "You might ruin them!"

"How?" she asked

Well, I had been well trained by my mother. I said, "You can step in some manure and ruin your shoes, and you can get them on your pants!"

And Dorothy looked around our little apartment in Hot Springs, Arkansas—downtown Hot Springs, Arkansas—and said, "Uh, what manure?"

Well, my mother had drilled me on these issues, so I shifted ground. "You could tear your Sunday clothes on the barbed-wire fence!"

She looked around again. "Uh, what barbed-wire fence?"

This was not going well. I looked at her nervously and said, "You're not going to buy getting grease off the tractor on your clothes either, are you?"

"No," she replied.

And so began a process of several years in our marriage of one of us trying to convince the other that he or she was right about how we should dress for Sunday dinner at our house. After several years of fruitful and not so fruitful discussion, it began gradually to dawn upon us that our debate over Sunday dinner attire was simply the product of the way we were raised.

I'd been raised on the farm, and the very first thing you did when you got home from church was get out of your Sunday clothes, 'cause you had to save 'em for Sunday night, and get into your everyday clothes. She'd been raised in town and often went out to eat at a restaurant. And she thought nothing at all of staying in her nice Sunday clothes through much of Sunday afternoon.

Well, we moved eventually into the stage of compromise. Boy, have we compromised. Now I barely get home from church and get all my Bibles and commentaries and books carried back into the house and there she is in her blue jeans and tennis shoes saying, "I don't think we ought to cook—let's just have sandwiches for Sunday dinner."

The most important times of our lives take place when we're in blue jeans and tennis shoes. That is to say, when we're at home and with our family when we're not trying to put up a front and dress nice and impress anybody.

The best times we have with our kids are when we're all in our tennis shoes and our blue jeans. (They're shorts now. That's a new stage I've not gotten to yet.)

And the most important times in our spiritual lives are not just at church but at the times when we kneel around a family altar in our blue jeans and tennis shoes at the end of an ordinary day.

You see, the church at Corinth seemed to have a Sunday clothes concept of the work of the Holy Spirit. For them the Holy Spirit was a spiffy thing, a spectacular thing, a dramatic and miraculous Spirit.

Those are words they would have used to describe His work—gifts of prophecy, words of wisdom, tongues, healings, miracle-working power, and all the kinds of things they thought about with reference to the Holy Spirit.

And the apostle Paul never contradicts any of that, never says to them, "That's false. That's invalid. That's wrong." What the apostle Paul does—and I think he especially does it in our text—is just to say to the Corinthians and to us, "The Holy Spirit needs to be at work in your life in the 'blue jeans and tennis shoes' times too."

The Holy Spirit needs to be at work in your life when you're not at church and dressed up. The Holy Spirit needs to be at work in your life when you're not trying to impress anybody— when you're just there and just you in the "blue jeans and tennis shoes" moments.

I think that's what he's saying in the text we've read together this evening. He says, "The Holy Spirit is writing a letter about Christ in your life"—in verses 1 to 3. He begins by raising this interesting question, "Are we beginning to recommend ourselves again? Do we need letters of recommendation to you or from you?" (author's translation).

Poor apostle Paul—what a time he had in that relationship with the church at Corinth. After he arrived there and planted the church, a few months later there were some people in it who were upset with him because he had not brought a letter of recommendation.

Now you laypeople may not realize this, but with pastors, letters of recommendation come and go all the time. I had to buy a new file cabinet when I started pastoring for all the letters of recommendation I was getting on evangelists and song evangelists before I realized there was another filing system in circular form that would probably work just as well. Those letters just keep coming, and they started in the very first century; you see the evidence right here.

There were people at Corinth saying, "He didn't bring a letter of recommendation with him!" Well, I don't know who he would have given it to, because there weren't any Christians—there wasn't even a church there when he arrived. But you know, it's a fascinating thing about some folks when they're upset about an issue—it doesn't matter whether it makes sense or not; they're just upset about it.

"Well," some could say, "he didn't need to bring a letter of recommendation to us; we weren't here when he came. But he should have at least asked for a letter of recommendation from us when he left!" Why? Who would he give it to?

But there were people at the church of Corinth who were upset with him because he'd not asked for that letter of recommendation when he left. And Paul says, "Hey, hey, hey, hey—letters of recommendation are not the issue of my ministry. You, church at Corinth—you, believers of New Mexico—you are my letter of recommendation, because you are a letter about Jesus Christ that the Holy Spirit is writing to the world."

That was a very significant kind of statement for Paul to make. You see, in the world in which Paul lived, a letter was a substitute for the presence of a person. Paul wrote letters because he couldn't be there. In fact, in 1 Corinthians, chapter 5, he calls for a meeting of the church board, announces the agenda, votes a guy out, and announces the results—all by a letter. It's the substitute for his presence.

You are a letter of Christ when Jesus cannot be present on earth anymore, because He's ascended to the Father. Part of what He wants to do is to write a letter that will represent Him.

And the letter He writes to represent Him—to be His substitute presence in the world—is you. Now that gives me some pause. If you and I are the letter that represents Christ in the world, what kind of thing is the world reading? What is the world discovering about Christ? What kind of letter are you?

As I pondered that question, my mind kind of drifted off to when I went to college. My folks drove me ceremoniously up to what was old Chapman Hall at Bethany. It was a guys' dorm. It was the one that didn't have any air-conditioning or anything else in it.

They drove off, and the last words my mom said were, "You may call us collect a month from now." My mother can squeeze pennies smaller than anybody I've ever met. She was dying to know what was happening in my life, but she wasn't going to pay for a telephone call. This was way back in 1968 when it probably cost two or three dollars. She wasn't going to pay for a call but once a month.

But I'd only been at school about three days when I got my first letter from Mom. Now I told you she kind of squeezes pennies. She doesn't use that wide-ruled stuff—she uses that narrow-lined stuff. Now, you know there's a little column on the side you're not supposed to write in? Don't tell my mom that; that's paper, and she paid for it. So she had written from side-to-side, from the top clear to the bottom—first page, front and back; and second page, front and back. Then about halfway through the second page on the back, it was obvious that she wasn't done talking to me.

But she wasn't going to waste another whole page on me, so she began to write two lines in every little space. And she told me what was going on at home. She told me about my dad and family devotions, about how he would pray until he came to pray for me and then would just start crying.

And she told about how after a while she and the kids would all get up and go to bed and leave him there to see if he could ever solve his problem. She revealed the heart of our family in that letter.

Not to be outdone, I got out my little Smith-Corona typewriter—the one I had gotten for college—sat down cross-legged (I won't show you how I sit down cross-legged on the floor anymore; I can't do that), and I wrote on my paper from side to side (a true son of my mother), front and back, and revealed the hurt of the heart in a boy at college. And every week, those letters went back and forth between the heart of a family and the heart of a son.

I think that's the kind of letter the Holy Spirit would like to be writing in our lives—that when the people of the world read us, they read not just information about Jesus but the heart of Jesus. It's the love of Jesus they discover. It's the warmth of Jesus they begin to pick up on.

And you know where that happens? It doesn't happen when you're at church. The world doesn't read the letter that your life is while you're at church. And while you're lifting your hands, clapping, praising God, or facing whatever you face, wherever you do whatever you do at church—the world doesn't notice it there. It's when you're at home in your blue jeans and tennis shoes.

Across the fence people notice it. It's when you're playing in the yard with your kids and how you talk to them that they notice it.

It's when you're in the grocery store late at night because you forgot something, or early in the morning because you forgot something.

It's there they notice the kind of letter about Jesus Christ that you are. In the "blue jeans and tennis shoes" moments of your lives the Holy Spirit is wanting to write a letter through your life that will reveal the very heart of Jesus to the world.

Paul says also that the Holy Spirit is wanting to make us adequate for ministry. This is the message of verses 4 through 6. Now the question of

Paul's adequacy at Corinth is more profound than simply that question of letters of recommendation going back and forth.

If you were to look back in your New Testament to chapter 2, verse 16, you would discover Paul raising another question, "Who is sufficient? Who is adequate for all these things?" (author's paraphrase). And if you look back to verse 15, you realize he is talking about his ministry of sharing the gospel around the world.

And he describes his ministry as being a fragrance of the gospel. But he says, "You know what? The fragrance of the gospel's an interesting kind of smell. To some people it's the smell of beautiful roses—the people being saved.

"But to some people it's the smell and stench of death—because some people accept the gospel and receive the beautiful fragrance of it, and other people reject it. And for them, that rejection becomes their judgment and their condemnation. And they will eventually die, and it is a stench then." And he says, "Man! Who is adequate? Who is sufficient? Who is up to the responsibility of sharing and bearing the good news of the gospel, knowing that people's eternal destiny rests upon it?" (see v. 16).

Well, he answers that question in our text and starting in verse 4 (chap. 3). In verse 5 he says, "Not that we are sufficient from ourselves to consider anything, any effect of the gospel is deriving from us. Our sufficiency, our adequacy, is from God, who makes us adequate to be ministers" (author's paraphrase).

Now it's interesting that Paul uses the "we" throughout here. I don't think he's just using the preacher "we." He's saying "we"—he, his readers, all of us. You see, when Paul wrote this, there weren't any ordained preachers. There weren't any full-time Christian workers. There were just Christians, there were just workers, there were just ministers, and there were just servants. And all God's people had then—and I believe all God's people have today—the responsibility of bearing the witness of the gospel to people's lives.

And some of you say, "Man, I can't do that."

I know you can't. Let me tell you something else. If you go to school all of your life and get a Ph.D., you still can't do it—because what makes you adequate for ministry is not education.

And you ought to know I believe in education and I think it's very important. But it isn't what makes you adequate for ministry—it's the Holy Spirit that makes you adequate for ministry. And a part of the responsibility that God places on every believer's life is to place himself or herself at the disposal of God. Whatever your education is—and you ought to be getting as much as you can—but whatever it is, you place that in the hands of God and you say,

> "Holy Spirit, I'm really nervous about this. I'm not adequate to stand in front of people at family camp and preach the gospel. I'm not adequate to tell my neighbor across the road about the gospel."

And God says, "Yeah, but My Spirit can make you adequate. My Spirit will work in your lives."

A few years ago a seminary student—during the class devotion time I always have at the beginning of class where I ask about prayer requests and praise reports—requested prayer in his own life. We've had a very strong evangelism program at Nazarene Theological Seminary for I don't know how many thousands of years. Chic Shaver has taught people to present the gospel, and seminary graduates know how to do that. And this seminary student said in class,

> "I want you all to pray for me. I've known I've needed to witness to a certain guy where I work. And I've seen the door gradually opening. . . . and all of a sudden last night at work, he just opened the door for me. And I knew right then it was time to share the gospel with him, and I froze up. I started thinking about my theology book and whether I could get it right, and this and that and the other . . ."

> You know, you don't have time to look it up in the Bible when the door opens for ministry. You don't have time to go look in the theology book or the how-to-witness guide.

When the time comes and the doors open, it's time to go. And it is only the Holy Spirit who can make you adequate. And you know where He does that? Well, it isn't in church. It's in the "blue jeans and tennis shoes" moments of your lives.

It can happen when you're there in the backyard and the barbeque grill's going and the neighbor drops by and just starts chattin' and all of a sudden you realize—here's a hungry heart. And in your blue jeans and tennis shoes, it's time to share the gospel. And Paul says,

> "The everyday work of the Spirit, the work of the Spirit in your

everyday clothes, is to make you adequate for ministry so that you can speak a word to people that brings life rather than death, because," he says, "you are made sufficient to be ministers of a new covenant, a covenant not of the letter but of the Spirit, because the letter kills" (2 Cor. 3:4-6, author's translation).

They don't need our rules, they don't need our regulations, and they don't need our laws; they need the work of the Spirit in their lives. And that will bring life to them. And it can happen, but it won't be at church—it won't be at camp meeting even. It will be in the everyday moments of your life—at the grocery store, in the backyard, at school—in the "blue jeans and tennis shoes" moments of your life.

Finally—(And you probably should know that the president of Bethany Nazarene College who hired me was Dr. John L. Knight; he's lived to regret that and quit that job and took another job so he wouldn't have to live with me on his faculty.

(But I learned something from Dr. Knight in his preaching. You know what he said it means when a preacher says, "Finally"? It doesn't mean anything at all.)

Finally—the Spirit sets us free to become more and more like Christ. Now that is the message of verses 7 through 18. You see, the whole purpose of the work of God in our lives is that we might share in His glory. And Paul begins talking about the glory of God in verses 7 through 12.

The Westminster Catechism, for example, tells us that the chief end—that means the real goal of people, the real goal of God in creating us—is that we would glorify Him and enjoy Him forever.

We were created to live to the glory of God, and we don't. Rom. 3:23 says, "All have sinned and are falling short of the glory of God" (author's translation).

Here (see 2 Cor. 3:7-18) he speaks of the veil that keeps us and God separated from each other. The veil is the symbol of sin in our text today. It is the veil that keeps us from experiencing the fullness of God's glory and presence. But that is not God's goal in our life. And as the text unfolds, he says,

"The Spirit may remove the veil. The Spirit who is the Lord can remove that veil. And the result is freedom" (vv. 16-17, author's translation).

I know that we as Nazarenes are very accustomed to wanting to talk about that freedom as freedom to behave a certain way in camp meeting. But that's not what Paul's talking about here. What he is talking about here is freedom to become more and more like Christ.

What he's talking about is freedom from the bondage and slavery of sin; freedom to be formed day by day, more and more into the image of Christ. Where the Spirit of the Lord is, freedom is there to become more and more like Jesus. And he moves on into verse 18 and he says,

"We all with unveiled faces, when the Spirit begins to work in our lives, He removes that veil of sin that separates us from God and God's glory with unveiled faces, as if in a mirror"—what a scary thought—that we have become the mirrors by which the world sees the reflection of God on our face. It is the Spirit that does that work. And he says,

"We are being transformed into the very image of Christ, from one degree of glory to another degree of glory" (author's translation).

Now he describes that change in a rather fascinating way—transformation. The Greek root he uses is the same Greek word from which we get "metamorphosis" or "metamorphic"; the word is *metamorphaō,* meaning transformation.

When I first discovered that, my mind went right back to eighth grade earth-science class. You can tell I'm a schoolteacher—I can remember stuff I studied in eighth grade. Well, part of the reason is I had a teacher named Roger—Roger Hutaberg.

Many of you have common names that ordinary people have, but not many people are named Roger. And for me to have a teacher that had my name and my initials—well, I don't remember what he taught, but I remember Mr. Hutaberg."

And I do remember that he taught about metamorphic rocks. Mr. Hutaberg said that limestone and marble were of the same chemical composition and that the only difference between limestone and marble is thousands and thousands of years of heat and pressure—volcanic kinds of pressure—that over that period of time transforms limestone into marble.

Mr. Hutaberg said that coal and diamonds were the exact same chemical composition. And that the only difference between a chunk of coal and a beautiful diamond was thousands and thousands of years of heat and pressure. It's a funny thing, you know—we seem to value the marble more than we do the limestone.

The state of Oklahoma—at least when I lived there—claimed it was the only state in the union that didn't have a dome over its capital. And the legislators lamented over that now and then. But it would be so expensive to erect this beautiful marble dome over the capital. So I wrote in once and said, "Why don't you make it out of limestone? It'd be a lot cheaper." Ah, I didn't even get a nice letter in return.

I suggested to my wife, "You know, our entryway is really gettin' kind of crummy. Why don't we use some inlaid limestone for our entryway?" I actually got a better mark on the everyday clothes when we were first married than I did on the limestone thing a couple years ago.

And when I was teaching at Bethany—maybe some of the ladies here who were my students were one of these—almost every semester there'd be some girl who usually sat in the back of the room but suddenly one day would be in the front of the room.

After a while, I began to figure out what caused the girl to move from the back row to the front row of the class, because right at the end of class she'd come up and start kind of moving her left hand back and forth in front of my face, trying to accentuate this one finger. And eventually, I learned to say, "Uh, what's up, huh?"

"Guess what?"

"What?"

"Last night, I got engaged. See the diamond my boyfriend gave me?"

Well, I didn't have my trifocals then, so I sometimes couldn't see them; they were fairly small. I was tempted to say occasionally, "Why don't you have him get you a coal engagement ring? You could have gotten a much bigger stone, and it wouldn't have been near as expensive." But though I'm stupid, I'm not that stupid! And I never did say that.

You see, we value the diamond. We value that which has been through the heat and pressure of the metamorphosis—the transformation.

The Holy Spirit is wanting to transform you into a diamond—into a marble quality kind of Christian so the world can actually see the message and grace of Christ in us.

And you know how the Holy Spirit does it? He hasn't got thousands of years, so He has to turn up the what? The heat and the pressure in our lives. And you know what we usually do when that happens? We come running to Jesus and say—in a frantic voice—"Oh, take away the heat, Lord! Take away the pressure! I can't stand it!"

And Jesus is trying to say, "I don't want a coal engagement ring. I don't want an inlaid limestone entryway. I want something valuable! I want something precious from my people!"

And that's why the heat and the pressure of the transformation is there. And you know where it happens? No, it isn't in church, is it? It's in the "blue jeans and tennis shoes" hours of our lives. It's in the everyday-clothes moments of our lives.

It is when we're under the pressure of work and family, and all the people around us are seeing us. It is in those moments where the heat and the pressure's on that the Holy Spirit wants to transform us from coal to be diamonds for Christ.

What would you like the Holy Spirit to do in your life? Are you willing to say, "O Holy Spirit, I'd just as soon be a coal kind of mirror to reflect Jesus to the world. I'd just as soon be the quality of lime, so I really don't want to get into this serious stuff of being like Jesus."

It's hard to believe you'd be at family camp if that was really the desire of your heart. I believe that all across this congregation we want to be like Jesus. And some of you are right now in the midst of that heat and pressure, and you've been confused and you're frustrated by it, and you wish it would quit.

But God is trying to accomplish a work of transformation in your life. He's trying to turn you into the kind of letter about Jesus that the world can clearly see.

He's trying to make you a diamond-clear mirror that will reflect the glory of Christ into people's lives.

He's trying to make you adequate for the next time you realize somebody needs to know about what it means to follow Jesus.

Let us pray

Father, I pray that Your Spirit would speak to us in these moments as we come to the end of this service. In some of us the desire to be like Christ is only a half-formed desire. Some of us are in the midst of pressure and difficulty, and we're not quite sure what it's all about. I pray in these moments that Your Spirit would speak to them—say to men and women and boys and girls and young people across this congregation—"I'm trying to shape you into a diamond for Christ."

And Father, as we open our hearts to You, create in us a deep, growing desire that our religion not simply be something that happens at camp and happens at church but something that happens in every moment of our lives.

And if there are those here who need to talk to You about it, who need to confess to You, who need to seek Your guidance, who need to open their lives to the work of Your Spirit, I pray that You would grant them grace to respond in these moments of singing an invitation.

5

OUR CONFIDENCE—
THE FAITHFULNESS
OF GOD

J. K. WARRICK

introduction and interview

For 12 years J. K. Warrick served as pastor of the College Church of the Nazarene in Olathe, Kansas, before his recent election in 2005 as a general superintendent of the Church of the Nazarene. He began preaching at age 16 in Redwood City, California. During college he held weekend revivals and spent one semester away from classes as an itinerant evangelist in Texas and Oklahoma. Although he served as a pastor most of his life, he said, "I always wanted to be an evangelist." His first church was in Caddo, Oklahoma. From there he went to Dallas; Midwest City, Oklahoma; Pensacola, Florida; Cincinnati; Indianapolis; and then Olathe.

When I asked about his use of 1 Thess. 5:23, a standard Holiness text, he said he preaches from this verse regularly in his own pulpit and in every revival or camp meeting. He went on to say,

The reason I preach from that text is that it brings two streams of thought together—that there is the necessity of a moment of sanctification but that that moment is only valuable as it leads into a life of growth, development, and movement toward Godlikeness. It's a powerful scripture for me.

Has that balance changed in recent years?

For years in our tradition we talked so much about the crisis of the new birth and the crisis of entire sanctification that we neglected the theme of prevenient grace and then the growth that takes place between conversion and the filling with the Holy Spirit. I think we neglected this to our detriment and contributed to a generation of misunderstanding about holiness—about this whole message of transformation and living with a repentant heart before God, about being willing to accept the ongoing atonement in our lives, about the power of God to keep us clean.

73

Does that include the need for confession?

I think so. Holiness people, at least in our tradition, have been afraid of the word "sin" (I still shudder sometimes when I talk about the sins of omission/sins of neglect). Yet I may say something to my wife, Patti, in a moment of frustration or anger—and I know when I say what I shouldn't say, but I say it anyway—and find myself needing to go back and ask for her forgiveness and then needing to repent before God. I'm coming, I think, to believe that the more we have grown in Christlikeness, the more we see what we need to do in our lives. There's a greater sense of humility and brokenness before God.

How do you think members of your congregation would define "holiness?"

It would probably be almost as varied as the number of people we have and the traditions from which they come. Most congregations today are so diverse in their theological traditions and understandings that I don't think you'd get a uniform understanding of holiness. Probably a lot of that's my responsibility. It's also just due to the times in which we live and how well people can articulate what they believe clearly and concisely.

How do young people in this college community respond to holiness?

Young people today respond to authenticity. If the language we use in preaching the message of holiness is not language that resonates with life, they're going to walk away from it. So they are freer, for instance, with the word "sin." They're freer to use the word "sin" than people of my generation. And that level of honesty and openness and transparency is a really healthy thing as long as we don't lose sight of the objective God has for us. Young people respond to a message that is real and that provides answers to the challenges of their lives—and I think the message of holiness really provides answers to the challenges of life today.

What is the greatest challenge to the Holiness message?

I come back to this word "authenticity" again—to preach a message not only with our lips but also with our lives so that there's some reason for people to believe we're telling the truth.

sermon: "our confidence— the faithfulness of god"

As we celebrate Christian holiness during the months of January and February, I want to invite you to visit the book table in Vanderpool Lobby. There you will find a number of good Holiness books to further enlighten you on this important subject:

▶ *A Love Made Perfect* by William Greathouse, former general superintendent.

- ▶ *Holiness in Everyday Life* by George Lyons, a professor at Northwest Nazarene College.
- ▶ *Security: The False and the True* by W. T. Purkiser—this helps delineate the difference between the Wesleyan-Arminian position about sin and eternal security, and the Calvinistic position.
- ▶ One of the best little books that I've ever read about holiness in simple language is H. Ray Dunning's book *A Layman's Guide to Sanctification.*
- ▶ *What Does It Mean to Be Filled with the Spirit?* and *The Disciplined Life* by Richard S. Taylor.
- ▶ *To Be Holy* by C. Neil Strait.
- ▶ *Holiness for Ordinary People* by Keith Drury—another excellent book in language we can all understand.
- ▶ And then a book, not necessarily about holiness as I'm preaching about it these days, but about holy living—*Dismantling the Myths* by Dr. Frank Moore. This is an excellent book with some great strategies for incorporating faith into everyday living, as well as an explanation of what it means to call ourselves followers of Jesus Christ.

Please open your New Testaments to 1 Thess. 5. I'll begin my reading with verse 12. And I'm going to invite you to stand with me while I read to you from God's Word:

"Now we ask you, brothers, to respect those who work hard among you, who are over you in the Lord and who admonish you. Hold them in the highest regard in love because of their work. Live in peace with each other. And we urge you, brothers, warn those who are idle, encourage the timid, help the weak, be patient with everyone. Make sure that nobody pays back wrong for wrong, but always try to be kind to each other and to everyone else.

"Be joyful always; pray continually; give thanks in all circumstances, for this is God's will for you in Christ Jesus.

"Do not put out the Spirit's fire; do not treat prophecies with contempt. Test everything. Hold on to the good. Avoid every kind of evil.

"May God himself, the God of peace, sanctify you through and through. May your whole spirit, soul and body be kept blameless at the coming of our Lord Jesus Christ. The one who calls you is faithful and he will do it" (vv. 12-24).

This is the Word of our Lord. Please be seated.

So many good things could be said about this New Testament church to which the apostle Paul was writing—this group of believers who had gathered in the name of our Lord, in the little community of Thessalonica. In chapter 1 of this book we are told that the gospel had been preached to them with power, with conviction, and with the Holy Spirit.

It goes on to say that after having heard the gospel, there was a tremendous response on the part of these people. They turned from their old ways of sin and gave themselves in confession and repentance before God and were "born again" or "saved." It was a great revival—tremendous changes took place in their lives.

Further, we are told they were tested in so many ways, and faced different kinds of persecution because of their faith. But their faith never wavered in the face of all that persecution.

In fact, so steadfast were they in their determination to follow Christ that Paul told them they were an encouragement not only to other churches but also to him in *his* sufferings (see 1 Thess. 1:7-8; 3:6-9).

When we talk about how to live a holy life—when we talk about living together in a community of faith—we often make reference to the church of Thessalonica.

Paul said so many good things about this remarkable group of people who had proven themselves in *so* many ways to be trustworthy with regard to the faith.

So I'm really surprised when I come to verse 10 of chapter 3 and the apostle makes this statement, "Night and day we pray most earnestly that we may see you again and supply what is lacking in your faith."

In spite of all the wonderful things he could find to say about this terrific church—it was such a source of encouragement to him—he felt this overwhelming burden and sense of urgency that he needed to come yet once again to them and to supply what was lacking in their faith.

Now we read on, beginning with verse 11 of chapter 3. And he helps us understand what this burden was and the concerns that he had. He says, "Now may our God and Father himself and our Lord Jesus Christ clear the way for us to come to you. May the Lord make your love increase and overflow for each other and for everyone else, just as ours does for you. May he strengthen your hearts so that you will be blameless and holy in the presence of our God and Father when our Lord Jesus comes with all his holy ones" (vv. 11-13).

Whatever else might have been involved in this tremendous burden—so great a burden that Paul felt constrained to return to Thessalonica to supply what was lacking in the faith of these people—we can *safely* say from *these* verses of Scripture that it at least involved two things:

> First, there was either a deficiency in their love or there was an impediment in the growth or development of their love for one another and for Christ. And second, there was a lack of strength in their hearts. In other words, they lacked the power within to be blameless and holy before God.

In chapter 4, the apostle begins to address some very *specific* problems of morality and immorality that were proving to be something of a challenge to the people. You might think that God had him write these words for the times in which you and I are living! In this chapter he finally says to them, "It is God's will that you should be sanctified" (v. 3)—the implication being that you are not *now* sanctified in the way he has in mind, but it is God's will that you *be* sanctified.

He goes on to say later in chapter 4, "For God did not call us to be impure, but to live a holy life. Therefore, he who rejects this instruction does not reject man but God, who gives you his Holy Spirit" (vv. 7-8).

> So there is a tremendous sense of urgency. Passion gripped his heart. He needed to go at least one more time to supply what was lacking in the faith of these terrific Christians and whatever else was lacking in their ability to continue to grow—to mature and to develop in love for one another and love for God. They lacked the power, the strength to be blameless and holy before God.

In chapter 5 he comes to this prayer with which he concludes this little letter:

> "May God himself, the God of peace, sanctify you through and through" (v. 23) or "sanctify you wholly"—w-h-o-l-l-y—or "sanctify you completely" or "sanctify you entirely."

> It's a bold and audacious prayer: "May God himself, the God of peace, sanctify you through and through. May your whole spirit, soul and body be kept blameless at the coming of our Lord Jesus Christ. The one who calls you is faithful and he will do it" (vv. 23-24).

In this prayer of Paul—in the context of this prayer, the historical context, in the words that surround it—we gain an understanding into what the sanctified life looks like. What does it look like if you live a holy life?

People are always wanting to tell us whether things are right and wrong. And in the Church of the Nazarene, we've tried over the years to articulate and to apply the Scripture to the world in which we live. And I might say we do that without any apology.

We think it's a very important part of who we are as followers of Jesus Christ. What does the holy life look like? It's not just some great emotional, overwhelming experience where we cry and weep and then live powerless with no impact on the way we conduct our daily lives. And so the apostle has painted a picture, a word picture of what it means to live a holy life—what the sanctified life looks like.

Go with me to verse 13 of chapter 5. He writes in that verse that the sanctified life is a life in which people "live in peace with each other." In other words, we never allow ourselves to continue to be at odds with a brother or sister or friend.

Now there may be an estrangement, but that estrangement is not on *our* part. We *never* allow that to go on. Whether the other person ever admits wrong or acknowledges wrong, that's not the issue. The issue is that *we* determine to live in peace with one another.

He says in verse 14 that we are to "be *patient* with everyone" (emphasis added); whether it's in encouraging them or whether it's in *exhorting* them. Or even in times when we are *rebuking* them and *reproving* them, we're to be patient.

In verse 15 he says that you never pay back "wrong for wrong." You never give what you get, unless what you got is good. You always give back good. *Never* pay back, not *seldom* give back wrong for wrong, but *never* pay back wrong for wrong.

In verse 16 he says, "Be joyful always." In verse 17, "Pray continually." Let your life be characterized by prayer.

In verse 18 he says you'll have a grateful heart. You'll live in gratitude before God for all He has done.

In verse 19, he writes, "Do not put out the Spirit's fire." ("Do not quench the Spirit" [NKJV].) I'm amazed sometimes that when God begins to move, when God begins to do things in our lives and in the life of the church, we try to put out the fire of God's Spirit—we quench the Spirit.

We let little things and we let peripheral things get between us. And we get in a snit about something, and we spread our snit to other people, and we tell everybody else how disgruntled we are and how bad things are and how terrible this is and how unjust that is and how wrong this is—while all the time the Spirit of God is trying to do something wonderful.

And we're all consumed with ourselves—in our own little world, in our own little programs, in our own little ministries, as if the world revolves around us. And we can't see the big picture, so we throw water on the work of the Spirit! The Bible says the sanctified person doesn't put out the fire of the Spirit with self-centered activity and thinking and words and actions.

"Test everything." Don't believe everything you see or hear. Test it.

"Hold on to the good. Avoid every kind of evil" (vv. 21-22). I really prefer the way the King James Version says it, "[the very] appearance of evil."

People are always asking me, "Tell me what's wrong with this?" Well, why not ask what's right about it? If there's nothing *right* about it, then it's *wrong.* Can we understand that? Avoid *even* "[the very] appearance of evil"—the very thing that might cast a shadow on our character, or cause someone to question our relationship with Christ; stay away from anything that *looks* like it might identify you with the world.

Well, that's a word picture of the holy life. People might say there's no way to describe it. Well, the Bible makes a pretty good attempt at describing it. That's not an exhaustive study, but it gives you a synopsis of what it looks like to live a holy life with some broad principles that can be applied to every stage of life and every individual's life.

Not only do we have a word picture about the life of holiness, but in the language of this prayer we gain some real insights into this work of sanctification.

Paul is very specific about what he's praying for. He says, "The God of peace, sanctify you [holy, completely,] through and through. [And] may your whole spirit, soul and body be [preserved] blameless at the coming of our Lord Jesus Christ" (v. 23).

To "sanctify" means to set apart or dedicate for the purposes of God. And over the development of that word not only did it come to mean "set apart," but because everything that's set apart to God must be clean and acceptable to God, it also came to include the idea of purity.

You might think of the word "sanctify" as the verb and the word "holy" as the noun. Whatever God sanctifies, He makes holy. A holy life is the life a person lives after that person has been sanctified. "May the God of peace himself sanctify you [holy]"—now Paul is praying here that God will give to His people a holiness that He decisively shares with them.

Paul is not praying that these people will *develop* into something, but he's praying that an event will take place in their lives; that there will be an experience of the grace of God—an identifiable experience—a point in time to which a person might be able to refer, perhaps a time and a place.

The Holy Spirit draws a person to such a time and place. He draws us so that we might bring ourselves in surrender to God. And it is the work of God to sanctify, to make clean, to set apart for His purposes and for His use.

Just as we are saved in the moment we confess we are sinners and repent of our sins and then believe on the Lord Jesus Christ under salvation—just so we are sanctified when we believe in the sanctifying work of the Holy Spirit, surrender ourselves entirely to His will, and appropriate His grace in our lives.

And we are sanctified through and through. He cleanses us from all that hinders—everything that is opposed to His work in our lives. He cleanses us from sin.

The chief impediment to righteousness is sin. And the chief difficulty we have in our lives is that we are born with a sinful nature. And it is the Spirit of God administering the sanctifying grace of God that cleanses us from the sinful self that forever leads us away from God. A holiness that God decisively shares with His people—but there's more to it than that.

There is a wholeness in which God *sustains* His people: "May your whole spirit, soul and body . . ."

What does the Bible mean when it speaks of the spirit?

Think of your *spirit* as that place where you identify with God. It's where you decide what's right and what's wrong. You might call it "the seat of your will"; sometimes we call it "the heart." It's the very center of who we are.

Think of your *soul* as that inner place in which you know yourself. It involves your mind and emotion and will.

Think of your *body* as the way you relate to the world
around you. It is through the body that we live out what we
are on the inside. Jesus said it is what comes from the inside
that makes a person clean or unclean. Whatever we do in
the body, we do because that's who we are and that's what
we are.

The prayer of the apostle Paul is that God—through the sanctifying work
of His Spirit—will preserve us, will sustain us, will maintain us, will keep
us in a place of consistent and habitual righteousness until the day of the
Lord Jesus Christ.

No, he's not praying that God would help us to be consistent one day
and then slip into error and sin the next day. He's not praying that God
would fire our hearts with passion and devotion on Sunday, only for us
to be cool and indifferent on Monday. "May your whole spirit, soul and
body be [preserved]," be kept until the day of the Lord Jesus Christ.

So there is in this prayer—the language of this prayer—the plea
that God will decisively impart to these people His holiness and
that God will continually sustain in them a wholeness.

Ruth Paxton says that sanctification is a step that issues into a walk.
Others have said that it is a crisis that issues into a process. But there has
to be a time when we surrender to God's sanctifying work and when we
yield ourselves to the continued work of the Holy Spirit. And that work
continues for the rest of our lives.

Finally, in the expectation of this prayer we find the ground of our hope,
the reason for our confidence.

Why do we believe that this is possible? Why do we preach—why do I
preach, why do any of us preach—a message like this? Why do we articulate a doctrine like this?

First, we do so because it is God himself who has guaranteed that
the work can be done. There's no way you and I can sanctify ourselves.

The only thing we can do is *consecrate* ourselves, and that's to
offer ourselves. But only *God* can sanctify. Only God can set us
apart as approved and cleansed for His purposes and His righteousness. It's up to Him to do that.

The second thing I find in this prayer is that the apostle is convinced that God has called these people to be holy. And his confidence rests in the fact that if God has called them, God will be faithful to sanctify them.

Our confidence to be holy people today is not based on our determination. You can't try real hard and be a holy person. You just can't grit your teeth and clench your fist and determine that this is the way it's going to be in your heart and life. We don't have the power to do that.

Only God can cleanse the heart. Only God can purify the conscience. Only God can go deep within us and set right all that is wrong inside of us. Only God can do all of that.

And our confidence is in *Him;* it's not in ourselves!

Our confidence is not in the fact that we may come forward to an altar of prayer and believe God to do something. Our confidence is in Him.

"Faithful is he that calleth you, who also will do it" (v. 24, KJV).

Here's a word picture of what a holy life looks like. Here's a prayer that gives us some insight into the desire of God to decisively share with us His holiness and then to sustain us in a marvelous wholeness in spirit and soul and body all the days of our lives. And here is the ground of our confidence: all because of Jesus, all because of the finished work of Christ, all because of the call of God, we put our faith in nothing else and *no one* else but Him.

"Well," you say, "Preacher, you know I love God and I tell you I'm doing my best. I really am. I'm trying everything. I'm just really struggling; I'm doing the best I can do. And some days, I feel so good about God and I feel so good about myself. And other days, I act in ways that make me wonder if I even know what it is to be a Christian. I say things to people—it's not just occasionally.

That's the pattern of my life. I'm in a terrible cycle. I don't know how to do it. I do destructive things. I do things that are *self*-destructive. I say things I know are hurtful and damaging to other people. And then I never go back and try to correct it. I just let it go. I'm proud—I can't humble myself. I don't know how to deal with all that. What would I have to do for God to sanctify me?"

Let me leave you with four steps you can take this morning. These steps are for those who know God through faith in Jesus Christ and who are striving to live for Him and to love Him. And you may be as terrific and commendable as these people at Thessalonica—but still, you're experiencing an inconsistency that troubles you and causes you to question at times whether or not you even understand the basics of Christian faith.

First you must believe it is the will of God. You must believe it is God's will that you be sanctified as it says in 1 Thess. 4.

Second, you must surrender your life to God. Romans 6:19 says, "Offer [yourself] in slavery to righteousness leading to holiness."

Third, you must separate yourself unto God. Second Cor. 6:17 says, "'Therefore come out from them and be separate,' says the Lord." And He explains a little more in the next chapter; verse 1 of chapter 7 says, "Let us purify ourselves [or cleanse ourselves or, in a sense, let us separate ourselves] from everything that contaminates body and spirit, perfecting holiness out of reverence for God."

Fourth, you must trust Him to cleanse your heart of all sin: "If we confess our sins, he is faithful and just to forgive us our sins, and to cleanse us from *all* unrighteousness" (1 John 1:9, KJV, emphasis added). How much is all? Well, it's pretty near everything. "All" is all—to cleanse us from all unrighteousness.

"May God himself, the God who makes everything holy and whole, make you holy and whole, put you together—spirit, soul, and body—and keep you fit for the coming of our Master, Jesus Christ. The One who called you is completely dependable. If he said it, he'll do it!" (1 Thess. 5:23-24, TM).

6

EXPERIENCING &
PROMOTING THE
HOLY LIFE

CLAIR MACMILLAN

introduction and interview

Clair MacMillan's Holiness sermon was preached at the Church of the Nazarene's 2004 Pastors' and Leaders' Conference (PALCON). Attended by pastors and clergy from across Canada, this conference was one of several held throughout Canada and the United States. In his soft-spoken, personal way he spoke from a manuscript. The thread that held the message together was a story from his childhood telling about the challenge he faced trying to explain holiness to a skeptical adult.

Clair is a wonderful storyteller. In our conversation he said that storytelling is the best way to communicate the Holiness message—"the power of stories," as he put it.

In 2004 Rev. Clair MacMillan was elected as the district superintendent of the Canada Atlantic District of the Church of the Nazarene and in 2005 was elected to serve as the director of the National Board of the Church of the Nazarene in Canada. He comes to these administrative positions following 33 years of pastoral ministry in Ontario and New Brunswick.

At the 2004 PALCON in Canada, you preached a message on holiness that was extremely well received. What were you thinking as you composed the message?

Yes, it was a unique preaching situation in that the target audience was largely a group of ministers that were reasonably well prepared theologically. I felt I had a little more leeway than in an average church congregation to deal with some of the more subtle implications of the doctrine of holiness.

What are those?

Perhaps "subtle" isn't the best word to use, although some have been largely hidden in recent messages, but one preached about in the early days was the doctrine of assurance—that a person could know through personal experience that he or she had a particular kind of encounter with God, beyond any doubt whatsoever, and was at peace with God and could come with all of his or her challenges before God and discuss them.

Do you think we've lost that?

I believe we have largely lost it.

What is the consequence?

I think we are a church of spiritually insecure people these days reluctant to talk confidently about holiness.

I'll never forget the personal story of your childhood experience. You were confronted by a skeptical adult expecting you to be able to define holiness.

It was interesting. Yeah, he was very skeptical—I found out later he was very familiar with our tradition but because of continual dissatisfaction chose to abandon it for a much more generic form of Christianity.

Are people drawn to holiness or are they running from it?

It's not received well because it's not presented in a way that is perceived to be attainable.

How did you communicate holiness with your congregation during your 33 years of pastoral ministry?

Through the power of stories. I made the message real—not avoiding the complicated and sometimes painful issues in preaching holiness, but communicating the life experiences of people.

sermon: "experiencing and promoting the holy life"

Let me tell you my story.

My first discussion of holiness took place when I was 11 years old. I had just resumed my newspaper delivery route after spending a week at Cedardale Nazarene Boys' Camp. Lacking any self-consciousness about the burgundy T-shirt I was wearing—the one with the gray oval camp insignia proclaiming "Cedardale Nazarene Camp: Holiness unto the Lord" —I set out on my appointed rounds.

My district manager for the *Ottawa Journal* met me at my pickup point with some exciting news: "People are starting to move into the new houses on Broadview Avenue, south of Carling. If you can sign up 20 subscriptions, I'll give you a new bicycle. It's a Schwinn!" The Schwinn was the holy grail of bicycles in 1958.

An hour and a half later, when I had delivered the *Journal* to all my regular customers, I began to canvass for new subscribers. I called on 11 new residents and made sales to 7. I was on a roll, already calculating the number of hours I would save every week using a new bicycle, when I strode confidently up the driveway at 789 Broadview Avenue. I glanced up from my reverie and found myself face-to-face with my next new customer.

"Hello, sir," I said, extending my hand for a customary handshake. "My name is Clair MacMillan. I deliver the *Ottawa Journal* on this street. I notice you've just moved in. Would you like to subscribe to the *Journal?*"

Slowly, very deliberately, he put his paintbrush down, placing it onto the lid that was resting on the porch beside the paint can. In virtually the same movement he shifted his beer bottle to his left hand, carelessly wiped his right hand on his shirt, and grasped my right hand in his.

He introduced himself as Winston Mackie—not his real name—and ignoring my question, he looked intently at my T-shirt and asked, "What kind of camp is that?"

"It's a church camp, sir. I was there last week."

"What church?"

"The Church of the Nazarene, sir."

"Never heard of it!" he offered, obviously proud of his ignorance. "What kind of church is that?"

The encounter took place 46 years ago, but every detail still leaps to my senses when I think of it. I can still smell the fresh paint—a vivid hunter green, I know now—that he had just finished applying to his front door; I still see the sparkle of the chrome tailfin on the new, two-tone cream-and-green Buick Limited, which dominated the driveway. I can still smell the stale odor of beer on the man's breath as he waited for my answer.

I had no comparative experience of churches, knew nothing of any denomination but my own, and very little about that. I answered the only way I knew to answer, the way my primary socialization had programmed me to answer:

"It's a Holiness church, sir."

"What does that mean?" he asked, in mild curiosity.

"We believe in holiness," I stammered, recognizing that my careless choice of attire had dropped me into water much deeper than I was prepared to deal with.

I had exhausted the depth of my knowledge of the subject. The category "a Holiness church" should resolve all questions and allow me to resume my control of the conversation so I could sign up a new customer and move a step closer to my new Schwinn. It didn't!

"Is it a Christian church?" he asked.

I nodded affirmatively.

"All Christians believe in holiness," he said matter-of-factly.

That was news to me!

"Are you a Christian?" I asked, somewhat incredulously, as I glanced first into his eyes and then at the bottle of beer in his hand.

"Of course," he replied. "I was christened when I was a month old and confirmed at 12 years. I haven't missed a Christmas or Easter since," he added, chuckling. His gaze had followed mine as I looked askance at his beer bottle.

"So, Clair MacMillan, what makes this 'Church of the Nazarene' different?"

I had no idea what to say next. He helped me.

"I see you've got a problem with my beer?"

I nodded my head slightly, afraid to let my eyes meet his. I had not been raised to be this confrontational.

"Is that what your church believes makes a person holy—not drinking beer?" he continued.

"Not just that," I said timidly.

"Oh! There are other things too? Let me see. This church of yours probably doesn't let you smoke, go to shows, dance, and the like?" he went on. "What about pool halls, bowling alleys, and bingo?"

I continued to nod my silent affirmation while he continued his exploration.

"And you probably go to church every week?"

"Yes, unless I'm sick," I agreed, starting to feel as if I was.

"And you pay your tithe?"

Again, I nodded in agreement. Suddenly I thought, for the first time, of the moral dilemma I would face if I earned the bicycle. A sum of $39.99 at Canadian Tire—that's what the Schwinn cost in the 1958 summer catalogue. It was equal to a $4.00 tithe and everything my paper route would pay me for five full weeks! I felt a cold chill descend on all my enthusiasm.

"Does your church teach you that if you do some things and avoid some other things, you'll suddenly be holy?" he inquired. His questioning had taken on a more solemn tone with each ensuing moment. He was no longer being frivolous; the mocking undertone had subsided. He was asking me a serious question.

What he said didn't sound quite right, but I answered as best I could. "I suppose that's something like what we believe."

I felt like crying. It suddenly seemed that my promised bicycle was slipping away, but even worse, I had a deep sense of uncertainty about what I really believed. Why, I asked myself, had I worn that infernal T-shirt?

"Is that what you believe or just what your church has taught you?" he pursued, gently but insistently.

I had never thought to separate those two issues. I had never been in a church other than the Church of the Nazarene. My father was my pastor; his father had harbored aspirations to be one. Our family affirmed all the church had taught me, but suddenly I knew they were separate issues. God's Spirit was now the Third Person in the interview. I was facing a question I had to answer. It would recur, I knew, as my life went on; but equally I knew I had to answer it right there and then.

"How old are you?" he asked, seeming to change the subject.

"I turned 11 last month," I replied, greatly relieved that the tension was eased for a moment. That was a question I could answer. I began to breathe again.

"Are you saying you'll never question all of those things your church has taught you for all the rest of your life? If you don't question them, will that make you holy? And if you do question them, will that make you unholy?"

Is that the measure of holiness? Just what do we mean when we say we are a "Holiness church"? And having said it, how does that distinguish us from other churches?

The word itself gives some insight into what we intend when we make a claim to "holiness" with reference to the church.

First, I would ask you to notice that the word "holiness" is a noun in English. To have any descriptive meaning, the compound noun "Holiness church" requires an adjective. I could preach the rest of my allotted time tonight about supplying an appropriate adjective—but I won't. That can be a subject for another time.

Second, it is important to note that holiness is a very popular concept these days. I did a bibliographical Internet search on the words "holiness" and "holy," and I found over 300 titles published in 2003 with one or the other word. When I broadened the search to include cognates and derivatives of the concepts, there were several thousand hits! Many people, tired of the jadedness of the modern world and of the misappropriation of religion to serve political ends, are longing for an objectively verifiable and subjectively satisfying experience with God. Holiness is the hot topic of the first decade of the third millennium! Since the word is used so widely and with such great popularity, it is important that we attempt to offer a clear understanding of what we mean as Christians when we talk of holiness. Again, it would be easy to spend the rest of the allotted time this evening exploring the meaning of the noun "holiness." I will not resort to a dictionary definition but rather offer a composite understanding, gleaned from our literature and the writings of others over the centuries.

I am willing to be somewhat simplistic on the matter, recognizing that a simple definition lacks much of the subtlety that has amused and perplexed those who have disputed with one another over the matter. I will offer as a definition of holiness "the condition of spiritual healthiness that characterizes a person's comfortable fellowship with God, based on an appropriate relationship with God."

Our theological tradition has characterized holiness as "perfect love," that is, "love at rest" or "completed love." What is of interest to people like us, who claim to have a particular "mandate for mission" based upon that claim, is how deeply and broadly the desire for this kind of altered human condition has gripped people in all churches in these early days of the 21st century! With such an evident and widespread desire for this condition that Christians call holiness, should these not be the greatest days in Christian history?

While most Christians agree on the character and desirability of the condition of holiness, there is widespread disagreement on two matters:

The first question is whether it is a condition available to people in this lifetime or merely, to paraphrase C. S. Lewis, a "shadow-land, a bright shadow of something eminently desirable yet unattainable that draws us toward God." I will assume, as expressive of our theological and ecclesiastical tradition, that the answer is a resounding yes; holiness, as properly understood, is attainable in this lifetime.

The second question is, "How do we get there?"
I'll not try to refute the personal testimony of anyone who has entered into that kind of relationship and fellowship with God. Christian literature is rife with such testimonies from men and women from many theological traditions who have "entered into that rest" we have called heart holiness. For example, I would refer you to a marvelous little book by V. Raymond Edman, *They Found the Secret* (Grand Rapids: Zondervan, 1984), for an assortment of such testimonies.
Some 1,600 years ago Augustine of Hippo observed that the human soul is restless until it finds rest in God. That restlessness is revealed in the variety of ways people through the centuries have advocated as the "way to holiness."

The words of Jesus, "Whosoever will come after me, let him deny himself, and take up his cross, and follow me" (Mark 8:34, KJV), make it clear that the way of holiness includes the renunciation of a shallow and sensual lifestyle.

An important part of our Nazarene tradition has been our emphasis on the spiritual discipline of moderate asceticism. Who among us, who has been around long enough, can forget the prayer and fasting charts posted in the vestibule of our churches, graphically announcing "who is with the program!"
Woe to the people who didn't get the "star by their names" in the weekly accounting. That notwithstanding, I need to remind you that self-denial, valuable as it is as an expression of our relationship with God, will not bring you into such a relationship.

Similarly, Jesus has called us to a life of action in His name. When He said to His disciples, "I will make you fishers of men" (Matt. 4:19, KJV), He announced that the life of holiness is a life of action, not mystical contemplation.

Our Nazarene tradition has affirmed this calling. Our World Mission program, Compassionate Ministries emphasis, and other expressions of Christian involvement in making the world a better place grow out of the kind of relationship we affirm as expressions of holiness. Yet we are quick to acknowledge that these and other similar activities are powerless to bring us into such a relationship with God!

Again, some people have promoted quietism as the way to holiness. Based on a misreading of the sovereignty of God, they have concluded all action in response to God is an insult to God's grace; there is nothing we can or should do other than "leave it to God."

As Nazarenes, we have been quick to affirm that there is "rest for the soul" in a righted relationship with God. Nevertheless, any human act of quieting the soul, whether through meditation, psychotherapy, music therapy, or any other technique, will not bring us into such a relationship. Our relationship with God is brought about in another way.

Perhaps the oldest approach to seeking an appropriate relationship with God is through legalism. The logic is that since God gave us a list of rules and regulations in Scripture (613 laws, according to rabbinical tradition), the only way into a relationship with Him is through scrupulous adherence to all those laws. If we violate any, willingly or unwittingly, the relationship is broken and our quest for holiness is void.

As Nazarenes we have never (until very recently!) been ashamed to say we have some rules for living. We have offered our General Rules and our Special Rules as guides to people in making moral choices consistent with our love for God; but we have never considered the keeping of these rules (or even the Ten Commandments) as giving us access to a relationship with God. We have declared that right living flows out of a right relationship with God, but it can never bring us into such a relationship.

Many people in all Christian denominational traditions have wrestled with the complexities of "work[ing] out [their] own salvation with fear and trembling" (Phil. 2:12, KJV). Recognizing the vagaries of life, the perils of subjectivism, and the fallen condition of the human family, most denominations have eventually settled for a less than ideal solution to the problem of holiness. In essence, they have said to their members, "Don't trouble yourself about holiness. Only the collectivity called the 'Church' can be holy. Trust your salvation to 'the Church,' let 'the Church' define you, live in fellowship with 'the Church,' and God will average it out and you'll be safe."

The daughter of a very close friend of mine has been raised in such a tradition. Her Roman Catholic faith has shaped her life, formed her values, and guided her choices. She's 22 years old, a student at a secular university, and loves God dearly. She writes poetry about her desire to know God, to please Him, and to follow His ways. She has not been rebellious or wayward, yet she has been denied any satisfaction from her devoutness. Her ecclesiastic belief system says, "That's all there is! The only way you can please God is by having a relationship with 'the Church,' but you can never have a relationship with God in this life. The only holiness available to you is characterized by a submissive relationship to 'the Church.'"

My friend of many years ago was right! All Christians believe in holiness; only it means very different things in different Christian traditions.

Augustus Toplady, struggling with the same range of conflicting views on how to fulfill this universal human need, the longing for a satisfying relationship with God, wrote in the familiar hymn "Rock of Ages":

> *Could my tears forever flow,*
> *Could my zeal no languor know,*
> *These for sin could not atone;*
> *Thou must save, and Thou alone.*
> *In my hand no price I bring;*
> *Simply to Thy cross I cling.*

Although our belief in holiness does not distinguish us from other Christians, our belief in how holiness may be appropriated does differ. While some people may have come to heart holiness through any or all of the above means, we believe that the Church of the Nazarene has been called to experience and proclaim entire sanctification as the more excellent way to the joyous condition of heart holiness.

For the first 35 years of his life John Wesley was preoccupied with a sense of despair regarding his relationship with God. The record of his quest can be traced through his abundant writings. His struggles and anxieties may not be easily explained or categorized, but they are remarkably similar to the list I recited a moment ago.

Wesley's anxieties over his soul took him through periods of astringent asceticism, frantic activism, despairing quietism, hopeless legalism, and troubled ecclesiasticism until the evening of May 24, 1738, when at a class meeting on London's Aldersgate Street he found himself a reluctant participant in another desperate attempt to lay his spiritual anxieties to rest. While listening to a reading from Luther's preface to Romans, he "found his heart strangely warmed and, in an instant, knew that he believed and was acceptable to God, not by works but by faith alone." Hear Wesley's own words describing that moment:

"About 8:45 PM while [the reader] was describing the change which God works in the heart through faith in Christ, I felt my heart strangely warmed. I felt I did trust in Christ, Christ alone for salvation; and an assurance was given me that He had taken away my sins, even mine, and saved me from the law of sin and death" (Journals and Diaries, vol. 18 of *The Works of John Wesley*, Bicentennial ed.).

Three years later, in 1741, Wesley published his sermon "Christian Perfection," announcing for the first time his newly experienced confidence in his standing before God. To the entire world, and to all succeeding generations of Methodists, he proclaimed that the way to salvation begins with justification by faith. This Pauline doctrine, long absent from Catholic emphasis (whether Roman, English, or Orthodox), that "by grace are ye saved through faith; and that not of yourselves: it is the gift of God" (Eph. 2:8, KJV). Any proclamation of scriptural holiness must begin here.

Today, if our proclamation of holiness is in trouble, it is over this issue. We have become so skilled at socializing people into the church that we are in danger of losing this essential characteristic of effective evangelistic Christianity. People we seek to evangelize, be it our offspring or our recruits, can buy into our culture, accept the Nazarene way, and seek to find a satisfying relationship with God without ever having to deal with the fact that all culturally transmitted religion is inherently self-justifying. The Nazarene way is no more satisfactory (nor more satisfying) than was Wesley's pre-Aldersgate Anglican way! Any attempt at proclaiming Christian holiness that begins anywhere but with justification by faith alone ceases to be Nazarene or Wesleyan.

Let me illustrate. I type by the biblical method—seek and ye shall find! I can't claim to be a typist, though I have struggled with keyboards these many years! My first encounter with a keyboard was disappointing. As an avid reader, from earliest childhood, I was struck by the possibilities a typewriter held. The pages in books I read looked to my childish eyes as if they had been typed. I sat down at my father's typewriter expecting the product of my typing efforts to look like the page in a book. To my disappointment, they didn't.

The left-hand margin was perfect! The right-hand margin was another story. Try as I would, I could not make the right margin come out straight. I took a page in a book and tried to type it exactly as it appeared; that didn't help. I added hyphenations, sometimes inventing new ones to make my efforts come out even, like the pages in a book. The task was impossible! It still is, with a typewriter.

All that changed with the advent of the computer. I can type a page (still biblically) and then press a button; the very instant I do, the margin on the right is in perfect relationship with the margin on the left. That button, or icon, is called the justification button. It actively does to the page of text what God does to the narrative of our lives the instant we come to Him in repentance and faith. The relationship is made perfect in that instant.

I asked a computer techie about this. How big a screen would you need to have in order for the lines of those margins to change in their relationship one to the other? Looking at me as if I had two heads he said, "You can project those lines to infinity in each direction and their relationship will never change. They have been justified."

The central truth of the gospel is this great and miraculous action of God! Our relationship with God is made perfect and permanent in an instant. We can get out of it, of course, in the same way our first parents did, by a willful, persistent act of rebellion against God. Nevertheless, the relationship is never in danger from our stupidity or weakness or faulty judgment or even our negligence.

When we speak of entire sanctification, we are not talking about a change in our relationship to God; we are talking about the fellowship that derives from that relationship. The relationship has been made perfect through justification.

Now, in this context, hear my text for this sermon from 1 John 1:

"We proclaim to you what we have seen and heard, so that you also may have fellowship with us. And our fellowship is with the Father and with his Son, Jesus Christ. We write this to make [your] joy complete" (vv. 3-4).

Paul's preoccupation in his writings to the Romans and the Galatians is with "legal relationship." Over the centuries, this has been the dominant paradigm in developing the analogies of faith for the Western Church.

John, on the other hand, focuses on the fellowship that derives from a right relationship with God. To read 1 John, thinking "relationship" causes the reader—or the student—untold confusion. The Eastern

Churches (and, not by coincidence, John Wesley) took John's viewpoint as their dominant perspective in talking about sanctification, including entire sanctification. "Because our relationship has been made right through faith," they said, "we can turn our attention to fellowship with God. We can't have fellowship with Him until we have been justified, but once we have been justified (by grace, through faith), our fellowship with Him becomes the means by which 'the blood of Jesus . . . [cleanses] us from all sin'" (1 John 1:7, KJV).

The important question, then, regarding holiness is not, "How is your relationship with God?" It is, "How is your fellowship with God?" If your fellowship is intact, you are being constantly cleansed from all sin; you are sanctified and being sanctified.

Our fellowship with God is dynamic, not static. It grows; it changes; it is interactive. There are times when God seems palpably near; there are times when God seems distant and remote. Those changes in perception of our fellowship do not indicate a change in the relationship.

There are times when the fellowship is strained, through misunderstanding or other human frailty. There are times when the sorrows of life or physical or emotional suffering make it seem that God is unreachable. Fellowship is two-way, by biblical definition. If our "sending or receiving" mechanism is damaged, the fellowship suffers; again, that is not an indication the relationship has changed.

God has "shouted our justification" at Calvary! He is inviting all sinners to come and be justified and is proclaiming this as loudly as He can communicate!

Our sanctification, on the other hand, is whispered to us. It is the intimate whisper of a fellowship that can be communicated only in the softest of tones. A shouting fellowship is no fellowship at all!

My grandfather and grandmother raised 13 children to adulthood. Grandpa was a forceful, opinionated man. Converted as a young adult, he was never quite sure about how to go about the project of fatherhood. He lived through the extremities of war and economic depression, coping with poverty and a lack of education. His love for God and his desire to be a friend of God never wavered throughout his years. Yet he never became a skilled communicator capable of expressing subtlety in his conversations with his children.

He loved each of his children dearly, all the years of his life. Some of them knew his love; others assumed his apparent harshness was a sign he had rejected them. One son left for World War II in 1940, convinced his father didn't care about him. He returned to Canada in 1945 and took up residence in a city 1,000 miles from where his father lived. He never wrote, never called, never made any attempt at contacting his father.

> As a child during the ensuing years, I used to go to visit my grandfather at his farm. When I would stay overnight, I came to know what to expect in the morning. At sunup the rooster would crow. Within moments I would hear my grandfather's knees hit the floor, with a thud. For a full hour he would pray, first for his children, each by name. What always amazed me was that he lingered longest over the son who didn't come home.

That son came back 33 years after he left. At the joyful reunion the father and son each declared the fear that had haunted him through the years; each thought himself to be unloved by the other, that he had irreparably damaged the relationship. The truth was that each longed for the fellowship of the other. The relationship was not lost; it was marred by miscommunication.

> When we first hear the voice of God we, like Adam in the garden, are afraid; our impulse is to hide from the stern justice of an offended God. His voice is a booming condemnation of our alien condition. That voice of condemnation is entirely gone after our justification (see Rom. 8:1). God never speaks to us again in that same way. He doesn't need to. We have been brought into this new relationship of grace.

The voice of God to His adopted children is the "still small voice" of the Holy Spirit. The Holy Spirit is the agent of our sanctification. He speaks in a gentle voice, wooing us, weeping for us, whispering the love of the Father to us. He does not shout; it is the gentle voice of One cultivating a fellowship of perfect trust. Our first responses to the voice of the Spirit are cautious.

> It sounds so unfamiliar. But after our justification, as we fellowship with Him, we discover we can truly trust Him with the deeper things of life. In our prejustified state we don't dare to speak of our inner struggles, our fears, our disappointments, our failings. After justification we find that as we confess those things to Him, He opens our eyes to our real character.

A moment of full surrender comes when His Spirit assures us that we can trust *all* to Him. We have fellowshipped long enough with Him to know that as redeemed and justified children, we can—and must—discuss our entire being with Him. In that moment of full surrender, we enter into spiritual rest! We call that rest *holiness*.

Here's my question: Have you found that rest we call holiness? It comes only to those who have been justified by grace, through faith alone; it comes to those who are willing to fellowship with God and learn of Him through the Holy Spirit.

Let's go back to my childhood inquisitor—Winston Mackie and his question about holiness.

I knew only one way to answer. I'd had a sensitive conscience from my earliest childhood. I had no illusions about my potential for being holy according to the terms in which he had framed it.

I said, "I confessed my sins to Jesus at camp last week and asked Him to come into my life. I want it to continue throughout my whole life. As far as I know, I will always want to go to church and pay my tithe; I don't want to drink beer or smoke or do the other things my family has taught me to avoid. I don't think that makes me holy, but before I'd change my mind on any of it, I would want to pray about it and get Jesus' permission. I think that's what we mean when we say it's a Holiness church."

He fell silent. He looked at me kindly, and I think I saw moistness around his eyes. His final words that day still ring in my ears, "Don't ever be ashamed of your church, young man. I'll buy your paper; maybe we can talk again."

In the 46 years that have come and gone I've been asked the same question hundreds of times. In dozens of different ways, sometimes mockingly, other times in sincere inquiry, people have asked, "What does it mean when you say the Church of the Nazarene is a Holiness church?" Forty years of biblical and theological study and inquiry have not changed the essence of my answer.

I've never been ashamed of our church or its central message. Simply stated it is this:

We each enter into a personal relationship with God by inviting Jesus to be our Savior. We bring all the baggage of our previous cultural experience into that relationship. Some of that baggage is positive and constructive to our spiritual health and well-being, while some of it is negative and subversive. The positive habits and attitudes we bring to that relationship do not make us holy, nor do the negative habits and attitudes make us unholy.

If we were able to inculcate perfectly the positive values and behaviors of our Nazarene culture into our next generation, would we suddenly become a holy church? Or does our embracing of the term "Holiness church" impose upon us—or open us up to—something other than cultural purity?

As we become an international church, these questions press in upon us more insistently. Just as every succeeding generation of Nazarenes in the United States and Canada has had to "pray through" our moral dilemmas and embrace change in our collective ethos, Nazarenes in other parts of the world need to do the same. The Bible is definitive on the terms of God's universal moral law but in no respect defines the terms of cultural mores.

If you ever find yourself in conversation with the Winston Mackies of this world, do not be ashamed to tell them that your ability to be holy is a result of your fellowship with God in Christ as you commit to work out the behavioral implications of that relationship through the Spirit's direction and leadership. That is our hope, and by God's grace, that collective desire is what makes the Church of the Nazarene a Holiness church.

7

PRACTICE
MAKES PERFECT

MARK QUANSTROM

introduction and interview

Dr. Mark Quanstrom, professor of religion at Olivet Nazarene University, is the author of an important new book on holiness—*A Century of Holiness Theology*, subtitled *The Doctrine of Entire Sanctification in the Church of the Nazarene: 1905 to 2004*. For 23 years, following his graduation from Nazarene Theological Seminary in 1982, he was the pastor of the First Church of the Nazarene in Belleville, Illinois. His book was adapted from his Ph.D. dissertation at St. Louis University.

I wanted to know how a busy pastor could find time to write a scholarly historical study of the Holiness message in the Church of the Nazarene.

How do you integrate your research and scholarly pursuits with preaching?

When I came to Belleville years ago, I began graduate work in philosophy at Southern Illinois University and then discovered that St. Louis University (SLU) had a Ph.D. program in historical theology. I pursued the latter degree but not for the sake of the possibility of teaching. I went to SLU because I thought that pastoral ministry demanded a disciplined life of study.

How do you present this in your sermons?

Well, that was another challenge I wanted to embrace. How do you move from the academic world to the practical, pragmatic, real-life world—the "lived world" of people who don't use language like that and don't think in those terms? You know, the intellectual discipline changes you.

99

In your sermon you talk about what we used to believe.

There's a lot of conversation about the legalism of the mid-decades of the 20th century and maybe even later on—the '70s perhaps. I'm sure that—let me say it this way—we may have become legalistic, but I don't think the early Nazarenes were legalistic.

In your book you track the changes in the church's course of study leading to ordination and its Articles of Faith. Wouldn't most Nazarenes define holiness by the General and Special Rules of the *Manual of the Church of the Nazarene* rather than by either of those other resources?

That's probably true, which is why our holiness was understood by those outside the movement as legalism rather than as something substantial or authentic. But in light of our accommodation today to the sinfulness of our culture—I mean, my people just don't appreciate that going to an R-rated movie might indeed be sinful; that viewing five seconds of nudity in an R-rated movie would be pornographic; that gambling might indeed be sinful, as you exploit the weakness and win at the expense of another; that buying the most expensive home you can might be sinful. I mean, in light of how accommodating we have become, I don't refer to legalism in the early Church of the Nazarene. They made authentic attempts to describe what it would mean to be holy—that you wouldn't really indulge yourself by being entertained in the theater for three hours. I mean, why would you do that? There are more worthy causes. And you really wouldn't spend money needlessly. Why would you do that with so many needs out there? A legalism becomes a legalism when the love is lost. And I think that's what has happened. I don't speak despairingly of the legalisms of the very early Nazarenes anymore. I used to, but I don't anymore. I think it probably wouldn't hurt us these days to embrace some of the legalisms. It might keep us from being contaminated.

How do you think your people experience and define holiness?

They know I am pretty conservative in reference to some of the behaviors a lot of people participate in without reflection. But in that sermon I preach holiness as a quality of relationship between persons—the fruit of the Spirit and the Beatitudes and that quote from Micah. So I preach it as the fruit of the Spirit. I preach it as a quality of relationship between persons and between us and our Heavenly Father. And I preach that to claim that one has been made holy is dangerous. The most holy people I know would be the first to deny it of themselves, for themselves. And the most holy people I know are the ones most conscious of their need for God's grace and most aware of their sinfulness. What I ought to be conscious of in my own life is my need for continued forgiveness, continued confession. It seems to me that Jesus' story about the publican and the Pharisee at the Temple is indicative of what holiness results in. It results in confession, the need for God's continuing grace in one's life, and a total rejection of any holiness accomplished on our own.

In your book *A Century of Holiness Theology,* you trace the two streams present within the Holiness Movement. Are the people you preach to aware of that divergence?

No, not at all. Some may be, but I didn't elaborate on it. Some of my closest friends would know about it, but most of the people aren't too interested. They don't know of the conflict in the church over those two particular understandings. They sure don't. To be perfectly honest, I don't think that's the point as far as pastoral ministry is concerned.

What is the point?

The point is for people to be pressing toward holiness—how He makes us holy is through grace. Our part in this is attendance to the means of grace—being where God is so that He can do His work in us.

How do you make a case for holiness in our kind of world?

The appeal to holiness as far as I'm concerned comes in the promise of deliverance from evil, that is, the freedom that is ours when we are no longer slaves to our appetites and our lusts, not just physical but also mental—greed, envy, and pride. And if we would appeal to the restoration of broken relationships as the promise of holiness, I think people might be more inclined to willingly practice what it takes.

sermon: "practice makes perfect"

Do you know what Nazarenes used to believe? Some of you know. Some of you have been around the Nazarene denomination long enough to know what we used to believe.

But for some of you, this is the first Nazarene church you have ever attended and so might even be hard-pressed to say what we believe now, let alone what it was we used to believe—

and also, for that reason, not really care all that much about what it was Nazarenes used to believe.

But I think it might be very helpful this first Sunday in Lent to be reminded of what it was Nazarenes used to believe.

They didn't used to do Lent. They thought Lent ought to be 365 days a year, not just 40. They wouldn't have understood denying oneself only part of the year.

But that's not what I was going to say about what Nazarenes used to believe. They used to believe a lot of things, rightly and wrongly, but what Nazarenes used to believe with all their hearts and were willing

to defend to the death if asked to and went to their grave believing—
do you know what we used to believe?

That God was bigger than sin! We used to believe that.

A couple of weeks ago, we sang a couple of Nazarene songs: "Called unto
Holiness" and "Love Divine, All Loves Excelling." And I spoke just two
weeks ago about what God's purposes for us were—that He was all about
making us like Him. Do you remember that?

That morning we read of God's description of the disciple. We read
that morning the Beatitudes. We read from Micah, which said: "What
does the LORD require of you? To act justly and to love mercy and to
walk humbly with your God" (6:8). Remember that? It's all right if
you don't. That was two weeks ago.

But I said two weeks ago, and didn't hear any argument from you,
that God was all about sanctifying us, making us more like Him,
which is why we sang "Called unto Holiness" that morning.

What Nazarenes used to believe—the most important thing they used to
believe—was that God was bigger than sin and that His desire is not to
save us in our sins but to save us from our sins.

Nazarenes used to believe we could be made holy! They believed in
Christ living in us, the Holy Spirit living in us, so much so, that who
we were and what we did was really God, Christ, the Holy Spirit, being
in us and acting through us.

We took seriously, 100 years ago or so, Peter's admonishment in 1 Pet.
1:15: "But just as he who called you is holy, so be holy in all you do."

We took seriously, 100 years ago or so, John's declaration in 1 John
1:8-9: "If we claim to be without sin, we deceive ourselves and the
truth is not in us. If we confess our sins, he is faithful and just and
will . . . purify us from all unrighteousness."

We took seriously, 100 years ago or so, Paul's prayer in 1 Thess.
5:23-24: "May God himself, the God of peace, [make you holy]
through and through. May your whole spirit, soul and body be
kept blameless at the coming of our Lord Jesus Christ. The one
who calls you is faithful and he will do it."

We took seriously what Paul wrote in Rom. 5:19: "Just as
through the disobedience of the one man the many were made
sinners, so also through the obedience of the one man the
many will be made righteous."

We believed back then what Paul wrote in 2 Cor. 5:17: "If anyone is in Christ, he is a new creation; the old has gone, the new has come!"

We called it sanctification. You have heard of that, right? We believed that God, who raised Jesus from the dead, could sanctify us, make us different, change us, turn us into people who looked like Him—who were loving and not hateful, joyful and not negative and foul, peaceable and not contentious, patient and not short-tempered, kind and not accusatory or mean-spirited, good and not evil, full of faith and not fearful, gentle and not rude or harsh, self-controlled and not subject to their appetites.

Now, I'm not making this list up. That's what Paul said would be the evidence of God living within someone. And we believed that God could actually make someone like that!

Let me ask you, would that help your marriage, to be married to someone who was loving, joyful, peaceable, patient, kind, good, full of faith, gentle, self-controlled? Would that be helpful?

How about at work? Would that make your work world a little better, if you were surrounded by those kinds of people?

Kids, would that make your life easier if mom or dad were like that?

How about church? Would it make church better if people who claimed to be Christian, that is, Christlike, were in reality like Christ?

Well, we used to believe that that was the possibility. We used to believe that God so loved us that He wanted to save us from all of the self-inflicted pain sin causes. We used to believe that God didn't simply want us to get to heaven but wanted a little bit of heaven to come to earth, in and among His people.

Do you know what Nazarenes used to believe? That God was bigger than sin, that God could whip sin—and do it pretty effectively here on earth.

We used to believe that the power of Christ was such that we no longer had to follow in the footsteps of Adam but could follow in the footsteps of Christ—that when Satan came, Christ in us could beat Him.

We used to believe that God could purge us from our sinfulness.

Now that's a rather audacious claim. Just for the record, we weren't the only ones who believed this about what God could do.

The Roman Catholics believed it too. As a matter of fact, they still do. Roman Catholics have actual saints. They so believe what the writer of Hebrews wrote in Heb. 12:14, "Make every effort to live in peace with all men and to be holy; without holiness no one will see the Lord," that they decided there must be a purgatory where this holiness was finally realized.

But in Catholicism, there are those who have attributed to them sainthood, holiness. Catholics believe it.

Some Anglicans believed it. John Wesley did. Methodists used to. The Eastern Orthodox Church still does.

So this idea that God really could make us like Him was not some odd and sectarian belief. This was something believed for most of the Church's history, in mainstream Christianity. And to believe that God didn't expect a person to become holy was unheard of.

Do you know what Nazarenes used to believe? That God was very interested in our sanctification and that that was finally what He was most interested in. He wasn't simply interested in taking a bunch of sinning sinners to heaven. He was interested in getting the sin out of the sinners before He took them to heaven.

That was a pretty powerful message—that God could change people so they didn't suffer from their self-inflicted sinfulness—why, that was a pretty powerful message.

That God could take those destructive attitudes and behaviors that inflict so much pain on others and the world and replace them with attitudes and behaviors that were healing and wholesome—why, that was a pretty powerful message.

That God could take a lousy marriage and make it right—why, that was a pretty powerful message. People were looking for that kind of gospel.

That God could save a family—why, that was a pretty powerful message. People were looking for that kind of gospel.

That God could restore broken relationships—why, that was a pretty powerful message. People were looking for that kind of gospel.

That God could turn someone who lived like the devil into someone who could live like Christ—why, that was a message worth proclaiming. People were looking for that kind of gospel.

The early Nazarenes just didn't think they ought to put a limit on the possibility of what God could do in the mind, heart, and life of the believer.

Sin? As General McAuliffe said in the Battle of Bastogne when asked to surrender by the Nazis, "Nuts." God's bigger. He doesn't save you in it. He saves you from it. He can actually make someone reflect His holiness.

And they dared others to say otherwise. They dared others to say that the God who created all things and who raised Jesus from the dead couldn't do it. Well, that's what Nazarenes used to believe.

Can you imagine anyone believing that God could make us like Him? In spite of what the Scriptures say and in spite of what the church tradition says, it's hard to believe.

So there is a lot of conversation in the Church of the Nazarene as to why so many aren't so confident about the possibility. There's a lot of conversation in the Church of the Nazarene as to why it isn't proclaimed so much anymore. The question the Church of the Nazarene is asking is, "What happened in 100 years to make us lose the hope of the possibility?"

Now we still believe the Bible calls us to holiness. It's pretty hard to argue with the Bible. So what happened?

There are lots of reasons. I wrote a book about it. Have I mentioned that before? I just came back from a theological discussion group in Kansas City where 16 of us, why, that's all we talked about. A general superintendent was there. The president of the seminary was there. The holiness theology professor from seminary was there. Chairs of departments of religion from two of our schools were there. There were a lot of big-deal people—and me.

Two hundred and fifty of us got together back in December to talk about it. Three hundred people from all over the world gathered in Guatemala to talk about it two years ago. There's an online discussion group of 70 teachers, pastors, and church leaders talking about it.

Many people in the Church of the Nazarene are talking about why we don't seem to believe, at least as much as we used to, in what God could accomplish in our lives so we can experience, as the apostle Paul says in Galatians, the fruit of God's Holy Spirit living within us: Loving and full of joy and full of peace and patient and kind and good and full of faith and gentle and in control of our appetites.

I mean, wouldn't it be great if He could, really, change us? Wouldn't you like to be changed?

Well, I have come to a conclusion as to why we don't believe it as much or experience it as much. I think I know what has changed. And it is this—we don't do what it takes. Our practices have changed. We don't do the same things Nazarenes did 100 years ago. We don't pray as much. We don't fast as much. We don't go to church as much. We don't give as much. We don't deny ourselves as much. We don't separate ourselves from sin as much. And for those reasons, we don't see God's work in us as much.

What do you think? Does that sound reasonable? I'm thinking that if we spent more time in authentic prayer, if we indulged ourselves less, if we spent more time reading His Word, if we spent more time in fellowship with believers, if we refused to contaminate ourselves with the sin of our culture, then maybe we might see more evidence of the life of God within us.

So what's prompting this message this morning? Is it just that I got back from Kansas City on Tuesday and this is what's on my mind? That is probably a part of it but not the main part.

Do you know what is prompting this message? Lent is prompting this message. The gospel is prompting this message. And a sermon I read in preparation today is prompting this message.

Prior to the beginning of Jesus' ministry, immediately following His baptism, the Bible tells us the Holy Spirit led Jesus into the wilderness. Luke says the Holy Spirit compelled Jesus to go into the wilderness, where for 40 days—that is, where for a long time—Jesus prayed and fasted and was tested. Before Jesus began His life's mission and prior to the testing, He, the Son of God, spent 40 days in prayer and fasting.

Is it too much to say that He did this in order to increase His endurance, in order to make rock hard His faith, so that He might be victorious over the test.

He fasted and prayed 40 days before He was tested and before He would begin His ministry. And I remembered that this was Jesus' habit. Before every decision or momentous event, He prayed. He gathered with His disciples. He did church.

Before selecting the 12 disciples, Luke tells us He spent the night in prayer. Before heading to Jerusalem, Luke tells us He went up on a mountain to be with His Father and Elijah and Moses, bringing along His closest disciples. Before heading to the Cross, He went to a garden, with His closest disciples, to pray.

There was in the Son of God himself a need to pray and fast and fellowship. And you get the sense that these acts of devotion were not superfluous. You get the sense that they were absolutely necessary for the life of God within Him.

And a Baptist preacher, not Nazarene, commenting on Lent and the gospel, wrote these words:

"If you were to ask me where I am spiritually weakest, it would not take me a single breath to tell you that I, too, often substitute practical busy-ness for prayerful business. . . . I don't want to practice spiritual disciplines most days any more than I want to get up at 5:30 to run. I don't want to be still and quiet and unproductive. *I want the gain without the pain,* the gold medal without the training. I would rather rely on my gifts than on the giver of them."

And then he wrote:

"There are no shortcuts to spiritual fitness. You can't take a pill to adjust your spiritual chemistry. You can't lose forty pounds of ego fat in forty minutes a day by watching a video. It's more like the earnest martial art student who went to the teacher and said, 'I am devoted to studying your martial art system. How long will it take to master it?' The teacher casually replied, 'Ten years.' Impatiently, the student persisted, 'But I want to master it faster than that. I will work very hard. I will practice every day ten or more hours a day if I have to. How long will it take then?' The teacher paused long as if to calculate in his head. 'In that case, not ten years, but twenty.'"

(Rev. Dr. George Mason, "Training Days," *Day 1* [February 13, 2005], www.day1.net/index.php5?view=transcripts&tid=482)

Do you know what they used to believe in the Nazarene church? That God could really change us. That sin, those sins, such as jealousy, envy, greed, sloth, pride, lust, gluttony—that He could really and truly save us from them and fill our hearts with love, joy, peace, patience, kindness, faithfulness, gentleness, goodness, self-control.

That's what we used to believe. Granted, it's what the Bible says is a possibility—that God can sanctify us. And it was a powerful message. Who doesn't want to be saved from their ugliness?

Well, that's what we used to believe and because of that, there's a lot of conversation about what has changed and why we don't believe that so much anymore.

Here is my conclusion: It is not because we have misunderstood the doctrine. It is because we have forsaken the practice.

You see, we don't pray as much as we used to. We don't fast as much as we used to. We don't go to church as much as we used to. We don't give as much as we used to. We don't deny ourselves as much as we used to. We don't separate ourselves from the contamination of sin as much as we used to. And because of that, we content ourselves to suffer the ill effects of our sin our entire lives and we never discover the absolute joy of living Christ-formed lives.

In the Sermon on the Mount, in words that are really hard to believe, and pretty scary, in Matt. 5:48, Jesus said: "Be perfect, therefore, as your heavenly Father is perfect."

So here's the message in three words: "Practice makes perfect."

In the 37 days left of Lent, let's practice such that we might discover and receive all that God has for us and be truly changed.

8
THE LIFE & TIMES OF NORMAN B. ADAMS
BUD REEDY

introduction and interview

Bud Reedy is the senior pastor at the Stillmeadow Church of the Nazarene in York, Pennsylvania—one of the fastest-growing Nazarene churches in the United States. The growth of the church has largely been the result of his creative and energetic preaching. He speaks in the language of people on the street, in shopping malls, as well as in churches. He's not afraid to address the questions people have about religion—particularly about holiness.

And he's not afraid to take risks—as he did in preaching a series of 40 holiness sermons built around a story he composed. Each Sunday for 40 Sundays people came to hear another chapter in the story of Norman B. Adams. The story was filled with metaphors—easily remembered contemporary parables to illustrate the message of holiness.

I took the liberty to condense the heart of three of these messages into one piece, a chapter in the life of Norman B. Adams, with metaphors I'll always remember. I asked Pastor Bud about his life and preaching.

Describe your own ministry. Where have you been since you began, how did you get started, and where is your ministerial journey taking you?

I was born and raised in a little town in southern Maryland called Hollywood. Before I was born, my mother was invited to a Nazarene revival. She heard the message of holiness for the first time. In that service the Lord said to her, "This is what you've been searching for—that something that's been missing from your life. My mother continued to pursue the life of holiness and specifically the work of entire sanctification—that's why I was born and raised in the Church of the Nazarene.

How did you prepare to be a Nazarene pastor?

I attended Eastern Nazarene College and Nazarene Theological Seminary; had a couple of staff positions; and started the Church of the Nazarene in Hershey, Pennsylvania, in 1980. After this I spent a brief period of time in the youth department at Nazarene Headquarters; went to pastor in Oxford, Pennsylvania, in 1986; and then moved to York, Pennsylvania, my present assignment, in 1990. This means I've been at Stillmeadow now for nearly 15 years.

How has the church grown?

On my first Sunday at Stillmeadow we had 350 in worship, and last Sunday we had nearly 1,500.

What draws people to the church?

Well, it's my great preaching of course. No! That's a simple question, but I think it's kind of a complicated answer. We've worked real hard at being a values-driven church. We have identified our five core values, and we pursue those with a passion. And also we do not talk so much about church growth as church health. We want there to be healthy systems in place. A consequence of a church's health is that it will grow.

You use the story of a fictional character to carry a whole series of sermons. Who is the character and why did you use this approach?

I made a decision to preach a series of sermons on the work of the Holy Spirit in our lives—our everyday lives, our ordinary lives. And so I just decided, with my wife's prompting actually, to create a fictional character. We named him Norman B. Adams. The sermon series was subtitled "The Work of the Holy Spirit in the Life of a Person from the Moment of Their Conception Until the Moment of Their Home-Going."

You use a series of analogies to help understand Norm's story—the beachhead, a contaminated toxic-waste dump in his backyard, and his mother's dialysis treatments.

We were trying to find creative ways to express the doctrine of entire sanctification—being filled with the Holy Spirit and the Holy Spirit's work in a person's life—by using metaphors that people can identify with and understand. As the story developed, Norman discovered he had a barrel of toxic waste buried in his backyard. And it caused a part of his lawn to become discolored. It wasn't until that barrel of toxic waste was removed that the problem was really addressed in his life. And so the analogy is obvious—sin is a nature, and the work of the Holy Spirit we call entire sanctification is a radical treatment for the sin nature. So we told that story and used that metaphor as a way of making that particular theological point.

What about the beachhead?

The whole idea behind this is that an invading army must establish a beachhead from which it can begin a campaign to invade and conquer the entire country. So the idea is that when we are born again, the Holy Spirit establishes a beachhead in our life with the intention of invading, conquering, and eventually filling the entire country.

And dialysis?

Dialysis had to do with the purifying work of the Holy Spirit. Norman's mother was diagnosed with a kidney problem and went on dialysis in order to purify her blood. And that is part of the Holy Spirit's ministry—to purify us.

You really preached 40 sermons on the life of Norman Adams, and they were all on the work of the Holy Spirit?

Yes, at various phases of his life, different experiences in life. The one point I wanted to make is that God is at work in our lives. And so I just basically showed how the Holy Spirit was at work in Norman B. Adams's life, from the moment he was conceived in his mother's womb until his home-going, when Norman died and went to heaven. I'm not sure I'd ever preach a series like this again. It was a little risky. But I think our folks received it very well. In fact, by the time we got to the 39th and 40th sermons, we had some folks who said they didn't want it to end.

How do you think those in the congregation would define holiness?

Well, I think they would probably return to the metaphors I used. Because people tend to remember stories, I think they're going to associate holiness with those metaphors. And until people understand how the doctrine relates to their everyday life, I don't think they understand it. As I told this story-sermon, it helped them to understand the specific, very practical ways the Holy Spirit works in our lives. And I think they would remember the metaphors. They may not remember all the doctrinal points I tried to make, but they'll remember the story.

sermon: "the life and times of norman b. adams"

I am preaching a series of sermons called "The Life and Times of Norman B. Adams." I've created a fictitious character named Norman, and I'm showing how the Holy Spirit has been at work in his life, from the *moment* of his conception right until the moment of his death—his home-going.

Other characters in the story include Norm's wife, Wanda; his mom, Mary; and his pastor, Jonathan Cluett, at the Wesleyan-Holiness Church of Weiglestown, Pennsylvania.

As Norman comes to grips with surrendering his life to Christ and being filled with God's Spirit, we'll look at three metaphors that will illuminate his faith journey—and hopefully, ours as well.

Beachhead

Our Scripture lesson for the morning is the classic New Testament reference to the second work of grace we have come to describe as entire sanctification.

> "May God himself, the God of peace, sanctify you through and through. May your whole spirit, soul and body be kept blameless at the coming of our Lord Jesus Christ. The one who calls you is faithful and he will do it" (1 Thess. 5:23-24).

June 6, 1944—does anybody recognize that date? We now refer to it as D-day. The largest assault force ever assembled began to recapture France from the occupying German army. The ultimate goal of this invasion was to defeat the Germans and to liberate Europe from the iron grip of Hitler's Nazi war machine. The United States forces concentrated their efforts on two beachheads, one named Utah and the other Omaha, hoping to establish a beachhead there from which to launch their invasion.

> When the first wave of American troops landed on Omaha Beach at 6:30 A.M., the men encountered fierce resistance from the German defenses. The men of the 1st and the 29th Infantry Divisions and the Army Rangers encountered a wall of steel, barbed wire, and landmines along the 7,000 yards.

> > Try to imagine that—7,000 yards of the Normandy shore. From the bluffs overlooking the beach German-positioned forces raked the beaches with deadly machine-gun and mortar fire. The assault was stopped right at the water's edge for most of the morning, but the infantry refused to give up.

> The success of the whole invasion was at stake because if the American troops could not establish a beachhead in this area, a German wedge in the frontlines could divide the allied forces and put them at risk of a German counterattack. The Rangers broke across the sea wall and barbed-wire entanglements and braved strong enemy machine-gun and mortar fire to take the beach and then to take the pillbox-rimmed heights. They established a beachhead that day.

In this particular battle, a beachhead strategy was used. You say, "Well, Pastor Bud, I'm not into military science. What is a beachhead strategy?"

A beachhead is a position established on an enemy shore, a position gained as a secure starting point for further action. I guess you could call it a foothold, a place that allows the eventual occupation of an invading army.

Now, back to Norman's life. Years ago, in the fall and the autumn of 1969, Norman B. Adams ran his 1961 Rambler wagon into a tree on Old Route 173 near the Slippery Rock College campus. It almost killed him, but a few hours later he had another collision with another tree on a hill faraway.

He accepted Jesus Christ as his personal Savior, and the Holy Spirit established a beachhead in his life—a secure starting point for further action. You see, when Norman B. Adams was born again, the Scripture tells us he was born of the Spirit.

The Holy Spirit established a beachhead in his life and began a campaign to take over—to occupy every corner of his life.

The ultimate goal of this Holy Spirit invasion was not D-day. It was not just establishing a beachhead. The ultimate goal of this Holy Spirit invasion was V-day, total occupancy of his life, total victory, and complete self-surrender. I want to talk for a moment about spiritual V-day and what that involves.

First, spiritual V-day involves the total defeat—the total removal—of the enemy of our soul and his army from our lives. Paul wrote in 1 Cor. 15:56-57, "The sting of death is sin. . . . But thanks be to God! He gives us the victory through our Lord Jesus Christ."
Spiritual V-day involves total removal of the enemy.

Second, V-day represents the total liberation of Norman B. Adams from the presence and the tyranny of sin. It says in 1 John 5:18, "We know that anyone born of God does not continue to sin."

A beachhead is not enough. The ultimate purpose of the Holy Spirit establishing a beachhead in our lives is to totally liberate us from the presence of sin in our lives.

Third, spiritual V-day involves the total control of Norman's life. For where the Spirit of the Lord is, there is total liberation—there is freedom (see 2 Cor. 3:17).

Salvation is a beachhead; entire sanctification is what occurs when a person's life is totally under the Spirit's control, the total-and-complete occupation of a person's life.

> I know that the Holy Spirit has a beachhead in most of your lives, but let me pose a question, "Who is in control of your life? You or the Holy Spirit? Is your human sinful nature in control of your life, or is the Holy Spirit—the Spirit of Christ—in control of your life?" I'm glad He had the beachhead, but have you experienced total liberation?
>> Now some may ask, "I've given God a place in my life. Whatmore is there? What difference will it make to completely surrender my life to the Spirit's control?"

Let me answer by telling you a little about Norman B. Adams's life. The Holy Spirit definitely had a beachhead in his life, but the Holy Spirit did not have control of his attitudes, his emotions, his relationships, his marriage, his job, his finances—it was still all under Norman's control.

> But you need to understand something, we serve a jealous God. He wants total control of our lives, and the good news is that the Holy Spirit—once a beachhead had been established—began a campaign to totally occupy Norman B. Adams's life. The only question that remains is, "Will Norman B. Adams cooperate with the Holy Spirit? Will he surrender his life totally to the Lord?" That's the main question that is left to be answered.

Entire sanctification is what God does when we turn control of our lives over to the control of the Holy Spirit. Now I want to ask you a question this morning, "Is a beachhead enough? Do you want the Holy Spirit to take complete control of your life?"

In John 5:2-6 we find a really interesting passage:
"Now there is in Jerusalem near the Sheep Gate a pool, which in Aramaic is called Bethesda and which is surrounded by five covered colonnades. Here a great number of disabled people used to lie—the blind, the lame, the paralyzed. One who was there had been an invalid for thirty-eight years. When Jesus saw him lying there and learned that he had been in this condition for a long time, he asked him, 'Do you want to get well?'"

There is a very important principle I want to share with you this morning. If you forget everything else I've said this morning, please remember this—Jesus won't fix what you want to keep broken. Jesus will not occupy any area of your life unless you're willing to surrender it.

Entire sanctification really is God's response when we say to Him, "I want You to occupy every corner of my life." But He will not occupy any place until you surrender it. He will not fix what you want to keep broken.

So if you want to remain in control of your life, if you want to call the shots, if you want to stay at the helm, if you're OK with Jesus remaining in control of the beachhead only and you in control of an occupied territory, Jesus will not force His Spirit on you. But if you're ready to cooperate with the Spirit and surrender, victory is right around the corner. He will take over. He will sanctify you through and through. He will take control of your life, every square inch of it.

Besides a beachhead, another way of understanding holiness is through the analogy or metaphor of dialysis.

Dialysis

This truth is taken from Malachi, chapter 3, verses 2-4:

"But who can endure the day of his coming? Who can stand when he appears? For he will be like a refiner's fire or a launderer's soap. He will sit as a refiner and purifier of silver; he will purify the Levites and re-fine them like gold and silver. Then the LORD will have men who will bring offerings in righteousness, and the offerings of Judah and Jeru-salem will be acceptable to the LORD, as in days gone by, as in former years."

Norman's mom, Mary Adams, was diagnosed with lupus. And in 1981, she moved in with Norman and Wanda. Wanda felt she had to quit her job to care for Mary. And she did so for 10 years.

At first, it was simply a rash and some mouth ulcers that made her uncomfortable. But then she developed joint pain and swelling; mus-cle aches became much worse. Soon severe fatigue set in, followed by fever, headaches, bleeding gums, and shortness of breath. She began to gain weight. That was probably a side effect of the steroids. She had memory problems, which are common with lupus, although their cause is unknown.

But without question, *the toughest thing* about Mary's struggle with lupus was her renal failure—the reduced capacity of her kidneys to perform their function of filtering waste and toxins out of her blood. You see, your kidneys clean your blood by filtering waste and excess fluid from thousands of pints of blood. This process maintains the chemical balance your body needs to stay healthy and alive. Your kidneys also signal your body to make red blood cells, which carry oxygen to your body.

But Mary's kidneys weren't doing their job. Well, the Adamses did *everything* the doctor recommended they do. They monitored her diet, restricting the intake of proteins, potassium, and salt. They even tried to regulate her fluids as best they could. But, alas, the time came when all their options had been explored, and the doctor finally mentioned the word "dialysis." You see, there are two types of dialysis: there is "hemodialysis," which is performed at a special dialysis unit, and then there is the "peritonea-peritoneal dialysis," which is performed at home.

Mary's nephrologist suggested the former, and then referred her to a dialysis center, where she went every Monday, Wednesday, and Friday afternoon. They hooked her up to that dialysis machine, and the dialysis treatments were able to do for Mary what she was unable to do for herself—cleanse her blood and keep it clean.

Toxic Waste

At the same time his mom was undergoing dialysis, Norman B. Adams realized a problem was developing in his backyard. He had always kept a nice lawn. Yet, for some reason, one patch of it was yellow and brown, sometimes purple. He asked the ChemLawn guys to spray the problem area, but nothing helped. Finally, the lawn guys tested a soil sample. It was filled with toxic chemicals. A neglected barrel of waste was found buried three feet under his yard. Toxic waste was affecting his property and Norman didn't even know it.

Toxic waste, like any hazardous substance, can pose a long-term risk to health and the environment. It contaminates water, ruins soil, and pollutes the air. It can poison vegetation, animals, and people. It can kill.

After hearing a recent sermon by Pastor Cluett on sin, Norman realized that more than his yard was contaminated. He realized he was affected by something much worse, which polluted his whole being.

Norman realized he had a *sinful* nature. He learned that everyone is born with this sinful nature; it's inherited. You do not just simply learn how to sin and become a sinner. Each and every one of us is born with a sinful nature. Did you know that?

David said in Ps. 51:5, "Surely I was sinful at birth, sinful from the time my mother conceived me."

Ah, you've gotta be kidding! This cute, little, cuddly, chubby baby—sinful? Absolutely! You can't see it, but that sin nature exists in every child. And it's only a matter of time until each grows old enough to say these words, "Mine! No!" See? It is the contamination of the sin nature—that little toxic-waste dump that Norman B. Adams was born with.

Jesus, in Matt. 15:19-20, said this: "Out of the heart come evil thoughts, murder, adultery, sexual immorality, theft, false testimony, slander. These are what make a man 'unclean.'"

Norman's pastor, Pastor Jonathan Cluett at the Wesleyan-Holiness Church, preached frequently about a radical cleansing experience that the apostle Paul called entire sanctification.

Pastor Cluett preached frequently from texts like 1 Thess. 5:23-24, where the apostle Paul said, "May God himself, the God of peace, sanctify you through and through. . . . The one who calls you is [completely dependable; if he said it,] he will do it."

And after hearing about this work of entire sanctification, by faith Norman B. Adams asked God to perform a work of radical, comprehensive cleansing that included the toxic-waste site! And God did it! He was cleansed of the contaminating carnal, sinful nature he was born with. And he was filled with God's loving Spirit instead.

But as the weeks and the months went on, Norman was somewhat surprised to learn that the cleansing work of the Holy Spirit was not a "once and done" deal—not by a long shot! Just as Norman's mother needed to receive regular dialysis treatments to keep her blood cleansed, we need the Spirit's cleansing presence in our lives —continually.

Pastor Cluett explained,

"Norman, even though the sinful nature is thoroughly cleansed and your heart is cleansed of sin, as long as we are flesh-bound human beings with a *free will,* the possibility of sin remains. As long as you have a free will, you are going to be facing errors in judgment, temptation, and human frailties, and *all* of these things can contribute to sin—yes, even after the toxic-waste dump has been cleansed—because we still have a free will. We can choose to sin, to disobey, to rebel. That's why we need the Holy Spirit's continued, cleansing presence in our lives 24/7. He cleanses *completely* and continues to cleanse. It is both a crisis and a process."

Finally, Norman said, "You know, Pastor Cluett, I'm confused. Let me get this straight now; if the Holy Spirit sanctifies or cleanses us through and through, including the sinful nature, then why do we need to continue to seek His cleansing? Weren't we cleansed once and for all?"

"You know, Norm, that's a *great* question. Let me explain how I've come to understand the continuous cleansing of God's sanctifying presence.

"Number one, we need the Spirit to cleanse us from the *thousands* of times that we unknowingly fall short of His perfect standard. There are sins of *commission* and then there are sins of *omission.* And that's why we need the Holy Spirit there—to cleanse us.

"We need His Spirit to continually cleanse us of *every* thought, *every* attitude, *every* word, *every* deed that does not edify, encourage others, or please God. We need His Spirit to cleanse us from just the daily accumulation of dust we gather by simply traveling the road of the sinful world we live in.

"We need His Spirit to supply the cleansing necessary to live a holy life. And this life is *not* self-maintained! It is maintained only as I am in a loving relationship with Jesus Christ. I must stay connected to Him. Because after all, He is the Vine, we are the branches. And if we're going to produce fruit, if we're going to live holy lives, we must remain *connected* to Him!"

It was after this story that Norman was able to see the bigger picture. He realized that the Holy Spirit needed to clean up his toxic-waste dump and sanctify him through and through. As he reflected on his mother's kidney problem, he understood the importance of staying connected with God's Spirit—His cleansing Spirit—every day of his life. Norman understood that a life dedicated to God is not static! It is not a once and done deal! It is *dynamic*—the ongoing work of God's Spirit in our life! You know, gang—now more than ever we must remain connected!

Whatever it takes, stay closely connected to God's cleansing, sanctifying Spirit. He pursues you because He loves you. He wants to stay connected to you because He wants you to live a *productive* life. He wants to cleanse you *continuously* because He is a holy God.

And listen up, troops. Every time a holy God touches an unholy thing, it becomes holy. Every time a holy God touches an impure thing, it is made pure—it is sanctified.

Staying Connected

Let me ask you, are you connected? Or has there somehow been a disconnect so that the contaminating influence of our sinful nature continues. My challenge to you this morning—if you want to live a holy life—stay connected to a holy God.

Do you want to live a life that's distinctively different? It's important not only that He *entirely* sanctify you in a *crisis* moment but also that He continues to sanctify you as a part of a *process* He has begun in your life.

One Sunday morning Norman realized, "You know, God has been at work in my life and the Holy Spirit has been cleaning up my life, but I was born with a sinful nature."

Charles Wesley identified it as a "bent toward sinning," this tendency we have to sin. One Sunday morning it suddenly dawned on Norman, "There's my problem! That's the source of my contamination!" Pastor Cluett, because he was a Holiness preacher, began to preach about the sinful nature in every person and how the Holy Spirit could purify it and remove it and that only the Holy Spirit can purify his heart by faith.

By the way—I know this is not a sermon you will hear from every evangelical pulpit. In fact, most evangelical pulpits will tell you something like this, "Well, you're born again and the Holy Spirit establishes a beachhead in your life. But you know that toxic-waste dump?—that's there to stay, baby. It ain't going nowhere. There's nothing you can do about it. That sinful nature will remain in your life until you die."

My response to that kind of preaching is twofold.

First, how big is your God? Are you trying to tell me that after Pentecost God by His Spirit can't clean up that toxic-waste dump known as your sinful nature, your Adamic nature, your carnal nature (call it whatever you want)?

Are you trying to tell me that the Holy Spirit can't clean that up? I'm here to tell you that if that's what you believe, your God is too small. There is a radical treatment for the sinful nature. Now, gang, listen up—you don't have to live three steps forward, two steps back; two steps forward, three steps back; in constant spiritual conflict with the sinful, carnal nature you were born with. I'm here to tell you that God, by His Spirit, can sanctify you through and through without that phony heart; He can rip it out and give you a brand-new heart and clean you up.

If you want to keep living your life believing God can't do this, you go right ahead. But after 10 years Norman got sick of it. He wanted to live for Jesus and yet his sinful nature continued to contaminate him.

Second, I want to share with you that I'm glad I'm a Holiness preacher. I'm glad I don't have to preach some kind of defeatist Christianity where the best you can do is the best you can do—that "boys will be boys" way of thinking where the sinful nature is just going to remain there, so you just have to learn to live with it.

No—you don't have to live with it. Not while the Holy Spirit is on the scene. You see, you've got this God who loves you so much and who wants to get so close to you that He will start purifying your life. Every time He purifies your life and you draw closer to Him, there's a greater sense of intimacy with Him, until He gets to the backyard.

You have that moment in your life when you realize, "I've got a problem in my backyard." I've got some good news for you. God by His Spirit is so holy that He purifies everything He touches.

I'm so thankful for that day in my own life. I'd been a Christian for several years, but I got sick of the conflict. I'm so thankful for the day I prayed, "Lord, I got this toxic-waste dump over here. There's got to be a cure. There's got to be an answer.

When I turned the Holy Spirit loose in my life, He cleaned it right up, removed it. Now you can put whatever theological title on that you want—entire sanctification; the infilling of the Holy Spirit; the result of total consecration, total surrender; second blessing holiness. I don't care what title you put on it. What's important is that you experience it, that you can be as Paul reports in 1 Thess. 5:23, "sanctified through and through."

Choosing Holiness

One day Norman B. Adams prayed for God to do it. God did it. This is what the Holy Spirit does—He purifies common, average, ordinary people like you and me, making them holy, like totally.

Now I know there are some individuals here who have been saying amen all morning long because Jesus has already come in your backyard and cleaned up the toxic-waste dump. I've been getting a lot of yeses, yeahs, and uh-uhs.

I know there are some others here this morning who are saying, "Well, yeah, that's not the first time I've heard that sermon, but I'm not sure I totally agree with the theology of entire sanctification. OK. All I'm asking is that you give it serious consideration.

I think there's another group of people here this morning who've never heard a sermon like this before. You're thinking, "I thought Christians are destined to sin every day in thought, word, and deed. There was going to be this conflict, this Rom. 7 type conflict, in my life for the rest of my life."

I know there are several people here today who are at that point in their spiritual journey and you've never heard a message like this before. In fact, maybe you're feeling, "Wow, you really, really blindsided me with this. I need some time to think about that."

You do that. We don't want to force you into anything. But I believe there might be some who are ready. The Holy Spirit has been at work in your life. You realize you have a problem in your backyard, and you're getting sick of the constant conflict between this new life you have in Christ and your sinful nature.

It just seems like a fistfight in a back alley to you. It's just this constant tension, and you're sick of it, and you're ready to do something about it. Whoa, this sermon was really for you. I mean, this sermon was for everyone, but this sermon really is for you.

I remember how it feels to be at this point. Aren't you just sick of it? Aren't you just sick of being sick from sin? Aren't you willing to cave in? Aren't you at that point in your life where you're ready to collapse into the arms of a jealous God who loves you so much and wants to get so close to you that you'll become holy at His touch? Aren't you ready?

We're going to close with prayer.

122 dirty hands—pure hearts

Lord Jesus, this is a holy moment. We've been ignoring the problem in our backyard long enough, struggling to live the Christian life—hot one day, cold the next. We have been double-minded people, with one foot in the Kingdom and one in the world.

We ask You to forgive us of the sins we commit; yet our sinful nature contaminates us again and again. We have the same attitudes and think the same thoughts; we say the same words and do the same things; we develop the same habits, or we just trade one habit for another.

It's toxic, Lord, and we're sick of it. We're praying right now that Your Holy Spirit will come and do what only the Holy Spirit can do. Make us clean!

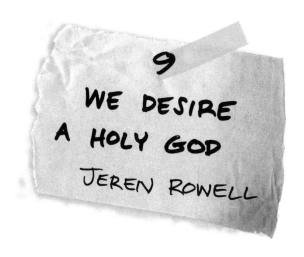

9
WE DESIRE
A HOLY GOD
JEREN ROWELL

introduction and interview

For 14 years, until his recent election as superintendent of his church's Kansas City District, Jeren Rowell has been the pastor of the Shawnee, Kansas, Church of the Nazarene. He also serves as the coeditor of *Preacher's Magazine*, a journal about preaching for Nazarene preachers.

This was one of a series of six sermons preached during a recent Lenten season as preparation for celebrating the resurrection of Jesus. In response to my question about the sermon, he talked about his effort to draw from a wide range of biblical resources rather than from just the "standard" Holiness texts.

Being able to preach on holiness in a series of messages provides an opportunity to give a much broader biblical picture. It allows me to go not only to the texts we might think of first with regard to Holiness preaching but to many other texts as well to show how holiness is part of the whole counsel of God.

I asked him a few other questions—when did you sense a call to be a preacher?

At the age of 15. I didn't really admit it to anybody—I was terrified at what God was moving me toward.

When did it occur to you that your call was to be a Holiness preacher?

I grew up in the Church of the Nazarene, so that's been my context and my story. It's the story I received from my parents and my grandfather, who as a layperson founded the church in which I grew up. So there's really never been any question about that. That was just a given.

How does the holiness identification distinguish your preaching?

The Holiness message really gives me something to say that's tremendously mean-ingful to people who are coming into my church week after week. They're search-ing for a place to anchor their lives—a way to negotiate life in this chaotic world of ours. The Holiness message is a hopeful, optimistic word to them.

Some of your message is about how the Holiness message needs to change.

The Holiness message, as I heard it, often got reduced to an exhortation about moral behavior. I came to understand that it's more than that—it's a way of looking at all of life and the entire world and how I live in this world.

In your sermon you mention that the song "Take My Life" presented a new concept about holiness.

That's right. I thought of holiness mostly as my obligation, something God expects of me, which it is, but the idea of it being my heart's desire, as the song depicts, was a fresh concept in my spiritual journey.

How do your people hear that?

I think they resonate with that idea. I think it speaks to something—a hunger in the hearts of people, at least in the place where I live and work.

How do your people describe holiness?

I think they would describe it as the essence of what it means to live out the char-acter of Jesus in the world.

How significant is the experience of holiness—or holiness as a religious ex-perience?

It's certainly something that we talk about and that people give testimony to in our congregation, even though my preaching and teaching focuses more on what it means to live the life of holiness than it does on a particular religious experience.

sermon: "we desire a holy god"

I invite your attention with me to the Book of Leviticus in the Old Testa-ment this morning as we continue to think together about God's call to holiness. It's our focus during these weeks—"Holiness: What Our Hearts Desire."

Leviticus chapter 19—we'll begin at verse 1.

"The LORD said to Moses, 'Speak to the entire assembly of Israel and say to them: "Be holy because I, the LORD your God, am holy"'" (vv. 1-2).

And then in chapter 20 verses 7-8, the Lord says:

"Consecrate yourselves and be holy, because I am the LORD your God. Keep my decrees and follow them. I am the LORD, who makes you holy."

I was about age 12 when I really started trying to figure it out. I was raised in the church, particularly in the Church of the Nazarene—I'm fourth generation in this movement. And I grew up in the church with a certain vocabulary.

I mean, we had a way of talking in the church using certain words that were peculiar to church. Just as I learned a special vocabulary for baseball, I learned a special vocabulary for church. In baseball, I learned terms like "can of corn," "gapper," "meat hand," and "a buck 57," which was my batting average.

In church, we said things like "Redeemer," "blood of the lamb," "salvation," "total consecration," and "holiness." "Holiness"—that one intrigued me, always.

Growing up in the Church of the Nazarene, I knew early on that "holiness" was a pretty important word to us. The saints of the church—in the little church where I grew up—when they said it, said it with reverence and awe.

Some, like Sister Garrett, sometimes wept when they talked about it. We sang of it at the top of our lungs, "'Called unto holiness,' Church of our God." We sang it like a march. And for much of my childhood, there was also a banner across the front of the sanctuary right above where the pastor stood to preach. And it had those words on it. You couldn't help but see them every single Sunday: "Called unto Holiness." There it was right in front of us.

The denominational emblem was printed every Sunday on the front of our bulletin. I remember sitting there, studying it and looking at it; "Holiness unto the Lord," it says.

And I remember hearing the words of this scripture we heard together again this morning. I mean, I heard these words pretty often. They were worked into a lot of sermons. "Be holy because I, the LORD your God, am holy."

Now, it seems to me there's not really a whole lot to misunderstand there; that's a pretty clear call. It was pretty clear to me that God was calling me to be holy and my church was calling me to be holy and my pastors were calling me to be holy.

But I knew me. And I wasn't real sure what holiness was about, but I was pretty sure it didn't look like me. I thought it looked more like old Charlie Griffith, Opal Mayhew, Mae Garrett, and my grandpa—but not like me.

So here's what I figured out—at age 12 I figured this out! Holiness was something that had to do with older people, who didn't really have anything else to do but sit and pray and read the Bible; they're the ones holiness referred to—not me.

Now, there was just one problem with that theory. I also thought my pastor was holy and he was only 29 years old when he came to be our pastor. So that kind of messed up my theory a little bit.

Rev. John W. Wright—he had to be holy 'cause whenever we had workday at the church, he'd show up in his wing tips, white shirt, and tie and work just as hard as everybody else. I figured he had to be holy to do that.

And I was in awe of him. I can remember so vividly going into his study at age 12 to ask him if I could become a member of the church. And he looked down his nose at me and scared me to death. I now know he was just trying to get me into his bifocals. But he looked down his nose at me, and he said, "Well, let's talk about that."

It scared me to death. That's all he said, "Let's talk about that." But I knew that somehow he knew every bad thing I'd ever done. And it's going to become the subject of our conversation. I was about to flunk out of holiness at age 12 right there.

And what I couldn't figure out about Rev. John W. Wright is that this holy man wasn't an old guy. He was a young guy, plus he was really good at baseball. I couldn't figure that out.

You see, the point is that having grown up in the church, I pretty much considered holiness to be a souped-up version of Christianity reserved only for people who had gone beyond the baser struggles and temptations of life. It was reserved for when you get toward the end—the really serious, the highly religious folks. They could talk about holiness.

I found out through my teen years and on into adulthood that I was really not alone in that assumption. Holiness to a lot of us seemed so unattainable. And so you know what happened? My generation began to change the language.

We modified the vocabulary. No longer did we want to talk about things like consecration, total surrender, sanctification, and dying out to the old self and holiness. We didn't want to use that language anymore.

And we wanted to talk about things like process, growing in your walk with Jesus, and becoming more Christlike. Not bad ways to talk at all. Those are great ways to talk about what it means to be a Christian.

But we've now come to a place in our only 100-year-old history as a movement, where "holiness" is a word a lot of our pastors don't even want to use anymore because it has, they say, too much baggage—too many negative connotations.

And maybe it does. I mean, I have to admit that in my own experience, it took awhile before "holiness" could be a loved and cherished word to me instead of a fearful and dreaded word.

Now fortunately—it's interesting—the next generation is helping us. They don't have all that baggage, 'cause we stopped talkin' that way. And so they recognize that holiness, like the Word talks about it, is a gift and not a burden.

They gave us the song we shared together a little bit earlier: Scott Underwood's "Take My Life." And you know something? It never would have dawned on me as a young person to think of holiness the way this song depicts it—as my heart's desire. I only thought of it as something being required of me and something that most likely I would fail at.

Holiness was not my heart's desire; it was my dreadful obligation.

Now there's no doubt, reading what we've read together this morning, that God is quite serious about this business of our holiness. And this word in Lev. 19 becomes foundational to everything else the Bible has to say, including what Jesus has to say about holiness.

The Lord says, "Be holy because I, the LORD your God, am holy." That is not a suggestion. That's a commandment. It's an imperative. *You be holy.* And it comes to us in the midst of a rather overwhelming list of dos and don't dos.

Chapters 18, 19, and 20 are full of that kind of stuff. It's a litany of wicked acts that are going to cut the people off from their relationship with God.

I mean, in chapter 18 it starts with the Lord saying, "Listen, you don't—you don't do what they do in Egypt. And you don't act like those people who now occupy the land of Canaan" (see v. 3).

And then a whole list of don't dos—don't do this and don't do that

and do not, do not, do not. There are 30 of them in that short
space. And then after what we read (chapter 19, verse 2), it starts
all over again, with do nots and the punishments associated with
doing the do nots, until we get down to chapter 20, verse 8, and we
finally read a hopeful word again.

Seems to me that pretty well describes how we have thought
about holiness. A good idea surrounded by a whole list of
don'ts.

But, loved ones—here's my essential plea to us today: Let's not miss the
point of God's call to us to be holy. Because it's really not about adherence to a list of dos and don'ts. What it's really about is recovering what
was lost when sin entered the world.

In Leviticus, the people of God are called to be holy, not because God
wants some arbitrary religious game to be played, but because God's
people are to be holy as God is holy. They're to reflect His image in
the world.

And when we talk about being called unto holiness, it's not essentially about behaving in certain ways. It's about the very character
of God who wants to answer our deepest heart's desire—the deep
desire we have for life to be made right again, the desire to really
experience deep, abiding peace again, and the desire to have hope
again.

So holiness isn't first about our moral purity. It's first about the
character of God. Holiness is not first about a list of dos and
don'ts. It's about being restored to the image of God. So let's
just put away the cartoon images of a sanctimonious person
wearing a halo and a prudish glare—our picture of holiness.

To be holy does not mean to be narrow-minded. It does not mean to be
primly pious. That's not essentially what holiness is about. It is rather
simply to imitate the very character and Spirit of Jesus.

To be holy is to roll up our sleeves and to join with God in what He's
doing in the world. And that's why I'm trying to say to us in this series
during this Lenten season—that holiness is not an add-on. It's basic to
what it means to be a Christian.

Because holiness is the one thing—the only thing—that will ever
bring that sense of wholeness and well-being to your life that you
long for. It's not about following a list of rules. It's about being
filled with the very presence of Christ himself.

So that everything I do and everything I am begins to be ordered by the Spirit of Jesus living in me.

Now, there's no doubt that God's standard for us is high. I mean, *Be holy as I am holy.* That's about as high as it gets. And Jesus didn't back up on that at all. In the Sermon on the Mount, when He was talking about how to live as a Christian, right in the middle of that thing, He says, You are to "Be perfect . . . as your heavenly Father is perfect" (Matt. 5:48). Yeah, right.

Here's the good news. Living up to that standard is not a matter of your effort. That's a good place to say, "Thanks be to God."

It's not a matter of your effort. Dare I say it again, it's not about you. It's all about God. And the heart of that good news is what we celebrate here. Every Sunday—Sunday after Sunday—what we celebrate is that whatever God demands, He provides.

He gives what He requires. He didn't just say "Be holy" and then leave us to figure out how to do that on our own. He said, "Be holy," and then gave us His Son to die for us, to pay the penalty of our sin, to provide the way that we can be reunited to God and have the image of God restored in us so that we can reflect the very character of a holy God in our lives. He does that because He wants the very best for us.

And in our heart of hearts what we desire, I believe more than anything else, is to be face-to-face with a holy God and not be destroyed—but to be loved and cared for and given His life.

The ache of heart that people all throughout our world are experiencing—the void, the emptiness they want so desperately to be filled—is all about holiness. You wouldn't express it that way, but we run all over the place and we busy ourselves trying so hard to fill that void, to meet that ache. And you know, our world presents us with so many options for doing that; we have a lot of choices to make.

And finally, nothing in this world will fill that void, that empty place, that ache like the very character of a holy God. Would you consider these questions?

Do you ever wish you could finally get on top of things spiritually, instead of feeling like a constant failure?

Do you ever wish you could be confident and sure about where you stand with God?

Do you ever wish you had the power to make the kind of life choices you'd really like to make—that you could really live the life you've always wanted and dreamed of living?

If those are your desires, then holiness is for you.

And for the next three weeks what I hope we can look at is very specifically what it takes to enjoy that kind of holiness God designed for us and calls us to.

For now, let's just remember these simple things—

God is holy and commands us to be holy.

God provides what He demands.

Holiness is a gift of His grace that's given to us.

It's given as a gift in a moment of just asking.

And holiness is a lifelong journey of becoming more and more like Jesus.

At age 12 I couldn't get it. But as I grew up, here's what I learned.

Holiness is not some special brand of spirituality that's reserved for supersaints.

Holiness is the regular pattern of God's people who just want nothing more than to live in relationship with Him and to have Him so fill us with His presence that we who have been separated from Him because of sin get to come home again and be restored.

So are you ready to go home?

Let's pray.

Father, thank You for Your call. And we're sorry that we have so often heard it as a list of expectations being placed on us. We heard it as a burden.

Would You remind us today that Your call to be holy is really just a call to come home and to have the deepest ache and longing of our heart filled?

Lord Jesus, please make us hungry to be holy. Please, by the work of Your Spirit in us, make us thirsty to be like You. And give us the grace, we pray humbly, to so surrender control of our life into Your hands that You can begin to make us into and restore us to what You had in mind in the first place—people who reflect Your very image.

Lord, continue to speak to us through the weeks of this Lenten season. If we remember together what You've offered, then what a great gift it is. Speak to us and help us to respond by opening our hearts wide to You and by allowing You to do the full and complete work of Your Spirit in us, we pray, in Jesus' name. Amen.

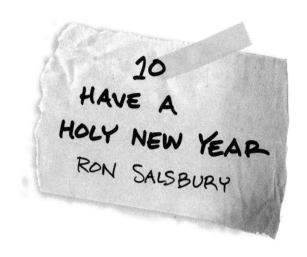

10
HAVE A
HOLY NEW YEAR
RON SALSBURY

introduction and interview

Ron Salsbury is pastor of the Pismo Beach New Life Community Church of the Nazarene, one of fastest-growing churches in the United States. During his 13 years as pastor, this church has grown from 900 to nearly 2,000 in attendance. Most of the growth is the result an effective appeal to unchurched, postmodern young adults.

As a former rock band leader he understands the use of music and the need to communicate in a way that attracts and holds the attention of people with little experience or understanding of the Holiness tradition.

We talked about his call to ministry and this New Year's Day sermon he preached in 2004.

When did you begin to feel a call to ministry and how did that develop?

I was called by God in 1969 to quit my secular rock band and start a Christian band, which I did in 1970 when I started J. C. Power Outlet. We traveled around during the '70s—the Jesus Movement era. Toward the end of the '70s I got involved in the singles ministry at Los Angeles First Church, under Ron Benefiel. I felt the need to go back to school and so went to Azusa Pacific University and then to Fuller and was ordained. I came in the back door, with all this as kind of a second career.

Where was your first assignment as a senior pastor?

I went to Lancaster First Church and I was there for five years and then came to Pismo Beach. I'm in my 13th year now.

Why do people come to your church?

Well, I think a combination of things. One would be it's a real lively place. The worship is celebrative. The people are very warm and welcoming. And we have a lot of fun, and also we have a lot of ministries to brokenness—we're a pretty touchy-feely place. We have a lot of recovery and support ministries out in the community.

How well do the people in your congregation receive the Holiness message?

I think pretty positively, because it's always couched within a passion to know Christ more intimately. It's a passion to know Him more fully and to love Him more completely.

In this sermon you reflected on your childhood experience in the Holiness tradition.

I'm sure it was my fault, but I grew up understanding holiness as being different. We're just to be different from the world and that's great, but why? Now I see that God wants to prepare us to make a difference.

In this sermon you used props—a water purifier, a blanket, and a flower bulb—to explain some fairly obscure theology.

I love to use props, humor, and stories and keep people awake the best I can. That's always been one of my gifts or abilities—to be able to illustrate something with a simple story or a simple prop.

And you used a clip from *The Lion King.*

Yeah! You are not yet who you are. So God wants us to become who He intends us to be. I think the story of Simba coming to realize that he is the Lion King and that he needs to practically appropriate what he positionally is, is true for believers.

sermon: "have a holy new year"

On this first Sunday of this New Year, may I ask you something? What do you really want in this New Year? What will make you happy? I recently read a survey that was published by *USA Today.*

They asked Americans, "What do you really need?" The response showed that most Americans feel overworked, stressed, and in need of more fun.

Now, you know, this may or may not be true. I hope you have more fun in this New Year. And I hope you have a truly happy New Year or at least stretches of the New Year that are happy.

But I want to say to you this morning that we all need something much more than more fun and much more than just happiness. We need a sense of fulfillment. We need a sense of purpose. We need to get up in the morning knowing that our life makes a difference and that we're headed somewhere. We need to know that we're doing something significant.

We not only need security in life—we need significance. And so I want to talk to you today about an old word in the theological dictionary we need to dust off and talk about. That word is "holiness."

What we need most in this New Year, I believe, is holiness.

When God was establishing His people right after they came out of bondage in Egypt, He gave them the Law—the Ten Commandments.

He also gave them directions for how they were to worship, with the establishment of the Tabernacle and the different sacrifices. He wanted to establish things with His people.

He said in Lev. 11:44, "I am the LORD your God; consecrate yourselves and be holy, because I am holy."

Now I don't know what you think of when you hear the word "holy." Maybe some of you think of a holy man—with crossed legs and a turban on his head.

Or maybe you think of somebody who is really old, so old that he or she can't have fun anymore, so he or she is "holy." You may think of holiness as some kind of restrictive lifestyle or being seriously out of touch with fun and fulfillment. But the truth is, the word here for holy in the Hebrew is *gadosh,* which means "sacred, dedicated, and purified." It really means to be prepared for something important—to be purified for a purpose.

Now I brought some props today—this is a water purification system, a portable one.

I originally bought this for my daughter who went on a mission trip to Nicaragua. Now it belongs to our son who's doing a lot of backpacking trips these days.

He's going to be using this to provide himself with drinkable water that is purified. I bought this for my daughter and my son so they could have purified water to drink. This takes out all the bad stuff so they don't get sick.

But the reason I spent all this money on this water purification system is not so my daughter and my son could pump some pure water and then put the water up on a shelf, shine a spotlight on it, and then every day go up to it and say, "Holy is my water!" No, I wanted their water to be purified so it would be usable.

The problem with holiness is that we have this lame idea that God wants to make us holy so we can be holy as an end in itself. It's really an issue of being usable. God wants us to be clean so He can use us. He wants to purify us so we can be used for His purposes, and that's what "holy" means.

In Heb. 12:14 it says, "Make every effort to live in peace with all men and to be holy; without holiness no one will see the Lord."

The word here for "holy" in Greek means "to be pure and unmixed." It was a word used in the ancient marketplace where on occasion there would be damaged ceramic pots sold by unscrupulous dealers. If they had a cracked pot, they would fill in the crack with wax. And so you'd look at the bowl and say, "Well, that looks good. I think I'll buy it."

But a wise purchaser would hold it up to the light and could see the crack in spite of the wax that was filled in, and they would know that that bowl was not holy, if you will.

And so "holiness" means there are no cracks, there is no impurity, that we are whole and pure and usable. "Holiness" means to be prepared or purified for the purposes of God.

Let's read Rom. 12:1 together.

"Therefore, I urge you, brothers, in view of God's mercy, to offer your bodies as living sacrifices, holy and pleasing to God—this is your spiritual act of worship."

You might circle that word "holy" if you're taking notes. That's the same Greek word in a different tense, which means to be physically pure and morally blameless.

In the Early Church there was a heresy going around that it really didn't matter what you did with your body as long as your heart was pure or your spirit was pure. You could be a believer and love Jesus in your heart and have the bumper sticker on your oxcart and the logo on your toga, but it didn't really matter what you did with your body.

And Paul is saying, "No way!" There is an integration of the person. We are holy in that we give our hearts to the Lord and we also offer our bodies—that we should be a unified package, if you will, giving ourselves to the Lord.

So holiness really is being different to make a difference.

I grew up in a culture that very much valued holiness. In the Nazarene tradition we kind of only got the front end of that thing. Our whole idea of holiness was about being different. And believe me, when I was a kid, I was different.

For example, I would go to school with a note that excused me from square dancing because my church didn't believe in square dancing at the time. And so I had a note: "Please excuse Ronnie from square dancing."

Now I got to tell you, I hated square dancing, so it was a blessing. And all my friends hated it, too, and they said, "Hey, can I join your church so I can get a note?"

Honestly, my idea of being a Nazarene was all the things we didn't do. People would say, "You're a Nazarene. What is a Nazarene?" I'd say, "Well, we don't do this, don't do that, don't do this, don't do that—we're different." But it never occurred to me that we could be different for a reason.

We are to be different to make a difference. Only God can do His work in us to really make us the right kind of "different." The King James Version says we are to be a "peculiar" people (Deut. 14:2). And the truth is, some of us are pretty peculiar even without holiness.

But I want to share with you today what holiness really is. And I want to do it by suggesting that just as a coin has two sides, there are two dynamics of holiness that are vitally important for us to understand. You have got to get this.

One side of holiness is what I choose to call positional holiness.

This is a matter of standing by God's grace. This happens when we're born as a child of God. If we'll accept His forgiveness for our sin, we come to a place where we recognize that we're sinners and we need forgiveness and we say, "Lord, forgive me for my sin. I put my trust in what You did on the Cross, Jesus, as the payment for my sin.

When that happens, you are instantly cleansed. Theologically this is called imputed righteousness. Imputed means that you are made holy by the grace of God because you are covered with the righteousness of Christ.

I brought some other props here today. I brought a blanket from my family room in my house.

This is one of my favorite blankets because it has all the different names of Jesus on it. Can you see them? Early in the morning I like to kneel down when I pray, because if I lay down, I would fall asleep. But I kneel down in my family room usually. It's dark and sometimes cold, so I grab this blanket and I like to cover myself in the names of Jesus. I think it's kind of cool. Let me show you.

You know, when I'm talking to my Lord and Savior, I just think about all the ways that He's blessed my life and how I'm covered with Christ.

When I'm covered like this, I realize I look incredibly silly, but the point is that this is what it means to be covered. And when we have the righteousness of Christ, that is positional holiness —we are covered with the righteousness of Christ. When the Father looks at us, He sees the righteousness of Christ and we are covered with an imputed righteousness.

We're covered by the grace of God, and we're instantly cleansed. And this is the holiness we are to possess and declare. We need to possess it, realize that it's ours.

When we have accepted forgiveness for our sin, we are now covered with the righteousness of Christ and we have—theologically—imputed righteousness. We're made holy. And we're to possess it and declare it.

First Pet. 2:9 says, "You are . . . a holy nation." That doesn't mean you ought to try to be holy, you ought to work toward it, or you ought to hope someday you will be. It says, "You are . . . a holy nation."

So that's why if you've accepted Christ as your Savior, you ought to be able to look in the mirror every morning and say, "I am a child of the most high God. I am righteous by the righteousness of Christ. I am holy."

The other side of the coin is practical holiness. This means that we're walking in God's love. It means not just that we're born as a child of God but that we're also growing as a child of God.

It means to cooperate with God's grace and to possess not just imputed righteousness but also—theologically speaking—imparted righteousness. It means that we're actually made holy, not just regarded as holy because we're covered with the righteousness of Christ, but that we begin to actually change.

It's like under the blanket we begin to change into truly holy people. And that's important. And so by God's grace we're gradually changed.

I have another prop here.

This is a flower bulb I borrowed from my wife's collection. Every December she puts these in little vases and she puts cranberries in here because it's very festive and red and beautiful for Christmas.

She puts these bulbs in the vase and then fills it with water, and the roots begin to go down and take up the water; then these things begin to grow a green shoot followed by little tiny white flowers that smell incredibly wonderful—they're called "paper whites."

I brought this as a prop to suggest that holiness is a matter of coming alive—it's a matter of something happening in us.

We're gradually changed as we grow in God's grace.

Now this, ironically, is one of the bulbs she did not put in a vase with water. And so it's just about the same way it was at the beginning of December. All the other ones came to full bloom, but this one didn't have the environment it needed to grow. It hasn't changed a bit.

And in the same way there is life in us, but we need to cooperate with God's grace in order for us to grow in what I call practical holiness. We need to commit ourselves to the disciplines of growth—prayer, reading God's Word, confession of our sins, and fellowship with one another. These are the disciplines of growth that don't come easy for any of us, but they're necessary for us to be changed by God's grace.

This is the holiness spoken of in 1 Pet. 2:11, which says, "Abstain from sinful desires." This and many other verses indicate that it requires our effort to grow in holiness.

Holiness is a journey—a process of growth by God's grace to become the people He's created us to be. Let me say it this way—to practically become what we positionally are.

One of my favorite Disney animated movies is *The Lion King.* Those of you who have seen it remember it's a story about the Lion King who has a little cub—a little son named Simba. The Lion King is killed, and Simba is banished by an evil uncle. He's in a far country. But he needs to understand that he is the Lion King, that he is the next king of the kingdom.

He needs to understand his true identity. He wanders around in a far country, confused about who he really is until he comes across a little baboon, a sort of holy man who is going to help Simba understand that he is a king, that he is positionally—if you will—the king. But he needs to practically become who he was destined to become.

Let's take a look at this scene from *The Lion King.*
[Sermon continues following running of film clip.]

"Remember who you are." That line from the clip is so important. If you've accepted Christ as your personal Savior, you are a child of God. You are a son or a daughter of the Most High God. The whole heart of holiness is remembering who we are.

The other line I love from that clip is, "You are more than what you've become." We need to become all that God is calling us to be. And so this is what positional holiness and practical holiness means—that we become who we are intended to be.

You are more than what you've become. Today I want to say that to all of you. You are more than what you've become. I'm not implying you're not where you ought to be. Maybe you're not; the truth is, we've all got a long way to go. But the good news is that by God's grace we can get there.

Let's talk about how we can live in this New Year—how we can live differently and achieve the practical holiness God wants for all of us.

I want to suggest *five things* from a passage in Colossians chapter 3, verses 1 through 17, and I'd like for us to consider what holiness will mean for us. In the *New International Version* this section has a title—"Rules for Holy Living." I don't think of these as rules. I think of them as a description of a life of holiness—the kind of holiness we want to pursue and develop in this New Year.

The first thing we see here in verses 1 through 4 is that holiness means living hopefully with an awesome future. Being prepared for something really important—that's what holiness is. Purified for a purpose.

Look at verses 1 through 4; it says, "Since you have been raised to new life with Christ, set your sights on the realities of heaven" (NLT). You might circle that phrase "set your sights."

In the original Greek it means to prepare for or pursue. It doesn't mean just to look at something and go, "Oh, that's nice." But it means more than just set your sights—it means prepare for and pursue the realities of heaven where Christ sits at God's right hand in the place of honor and power.

When we begin to understand our awesome future, it's impossible to not live with hope. As followers of Jesus Christ we ought to be the most hopeful people in the world.

When people look at our lives, they ought to say, "You know, that person isn't perfect, but I'm telling you that is one hopeful person!"

I can tell you during this last year I've had some times of real pain, uncertainty, and fear. But I'm here to tell you I've never lost my hope, because that is a gift Christ gives to us when He takes up residence.

The second thing holiness means is living confidently with a new nature. The question we have about holiness is, "Can we really change? Could Simba really become the Lion King? Can we as children of God really become the holy people He's calling us to be?" And the answer is, "Yes!" But we need to cooperate with His grace.

Look at verses 5 through 10, in Col. 3: "So put to death the sinful, earthly things lurking within you. Have nothing to do with sexual sin, impurity, lust, and shameful desires. Don't be greedy for the good things of this life, for that is idolatry. God's terrible anger will come upon those who do such things. You used to do them when your life was still part of this world. But now is the time to get rid of anger, rage, malicious behavior, slander, and dirty language. Don't lie to each other, for you have stripped off your old, evil nature and all its wicked deeds. In its place you have clothed yourselves with a brand-new nature that is continually being renewed as you learn more and more about Christ, who created this new nature within you" (NLT).

In other words, we are clothed with the righteousness of Christ, but now we begin to change by His grace because we have a new nature.

Now let me ask you a question. Do you think that we are what we do or that we do what we are? Do you think we are the sum total of what we do or that all the things we do really come from who we are?

Most religions say we are what we do. What you have to do is change what you do. So we have more rules and more religious effort.

We try harder to be better—we try to get pure. That's what we do if we are what we do. But that's not what the Bible says. That's not the message of Jesus Christ.

Jesus said we do what we are. What we do—what we say—comes from our heart. So, you can try to lop off all the evil behaviors you can, but you've still got an evil heart, and that's the problem. What we need is a new nature. We need to be changed from the inside out, and that's something religion can never do. What we need is a new birth. We need a new nature, and that's exactly what Christ gives us.

We begin to change from the inside out, and that's why we can live with confidence. You see, it's work that cannot be done without God, but it's work that God will not do without us. It's a partnership. It's important for us to work together.

I've got a couple of great quotes I want to share with you. One is from Mother Teresa. She said, "Our progress in holiness depends on God and ourselves—God's grace and our will to be holy. We must have a real, living determination to reach holiness" *(A Gift for God: Prayers and Meditations)*. She's talking about that practical holiness.

There's another great quote here from D. A. Carson—and this is a little bit long, but I want you to hang in there and listen because this is really good.

"People do not drift toward holiness. Apart from grace-driven effort, people do not gravitate toward Godliness, prayer, obedience to scripture, faith, and delight in the Lord. We drift toward compromise and call it tolerance. We drift toward disobedience and call it freedom. We drift toward superstition and call it faith. We cherish the indiscipline of lost self-control and call it relaxation. We slouch toward prayerlessness and delude ourselves into thinking we have escaped legalism. We slide toward Godlessness and convince ourselves that we have been liberated" *(For the Love of God,* vol. 1).

We don't naturally, without effort, grow in the direction of the person God's calling us to be. We've got to apply some effort.

Dallas Willard says that "grace is not opposed to effort; it is opposed to earning" ("The Apprentices," *Leadership Journal,* summer 2005). We don't earn favor with God. But we do need to apply some effort to grow in grace, to cooperate with what God wants to do in us, to develop this practical side of holiness.

The third thing—holiness means living freely with a new identity. If we're really honest here today, all of us will confess that there are times in our life when we find our identities in the silliest and shallowest of things. You know we want to be seen with the right crowd.

We want to wear the right clothes.

We want to drive the right car.

We want to be seen as successful.

We want to be seen as attractive.

We want to be seen as intelligent.

We may even want to be seen as spiritual.

We find our identity in the wackiest of things.

For Christmas this year Cathi, my wife, gave me a wonderful leather jacket. This is the coolest leather jacket, and I've got to say that when I have it on, I look pretty cool! It's extra cool when I put the collar up. I would have worn it and shown it to you today, but it's raining and I don't want to get it wet. What is it about leather that you can't get it wet? Can cows get wet? But anyway—I love this leather jacket, feeling cool, especially when I have my sunglasses on.

True story—last week I'm having my car worked on and at a dealership that's right across the street from another dealership that's partially owned and managed by a good friend of mine. It's a BMW dealership.

When I dropped off my car, I went over to say hi to him and he said, "Hey, do you need a loaner car?" I said, "Well, that would be helpful." And so he got on the intercom and he said, "Hey, bring Ron up a BMW X4." And he said, "Would this work for you as a loaner car?" And I said, "Ah, I think so. I think it will be just fine."

So, they bring up this hot little silver sports car convertible and I get in it and say, "Thank you. I'll try to return it," you know, "three years from next Thursday." And so I take off in this sports car, and I'm driving down the freeway, and I've got my leather jacket on. And I'm in this sports car, and I've got my shades on, and I look in the rearview mirror, and I start to laugh at myself because I'm looking way too cool.

And I'm starting to get caught up in this thing, you know, and I'm going down the freeway and I'm laughing at myself. I was so embarrassed that I took the sunglasses off a block away from the church because I was making myself sick. I didn't want people to see me and go, "Oh brother!"

Then I pull up to the church, and I get out of the car and it starts to rain. The winds start to really blow and I put my umbrella up. Do you know what happens when an umbrella goes upside down because of the wind? I realized when your umbrella is upside down, there is no way to be cool. You've lost whatever coolness you may have possessed!

I realized that afternoon that we get so taken up with external things. We spend so much of our life trying to buy the right clothes, drive the right car, have the right house and the right look and the right crowd to run around with, when our identity should really rest solely and safely in our relationship with Jesus Christ. That's what's really important.

Look at verse 11 here in Col. 3. It says, "In this new life, it doesn't matter if you are a Jew or a Gentile, circumcised or uncircumcised, barbaric, uncivilized, slave, or free. Christ is all that matters, and he lives in all of us" (NLT).

And so the truth is that if we're children of God, that is what should give us our identity. So if we drive a hot car, or a '78 Duster, or whatever we have, it doesn't really matter, because our identity is in Christ.

When you really get this, then you are really free, not only free to drive a clunker but free to drive a really nice car knowing that it is not the source of your identity. You get it? All right!

Well, let's look at the fourth thing that holiness means for us—living graciously with the motive of love. If we are holy people, truly holy, positionally and practically, then we are going to be gracious people. And our motive in life will be the motive of love.

If we have an awesome future and a new nature and a new identity, we don't have to live for ourselves anymore. Look what it says in verses 12 to 13: "Since God chose you to be the holy people whom he loves, you must clothe yourselves with tenderhearted mercy, kindness, humility, gentleness, and patience. You must make allowance for each other's faults and forgive the person who offends you. Remember, the Lord forgave you, so you must forgive others" (NLT).

Gracious living means that we afford to others the grace God has given to us, that we give other people some slack—we make allowance for their foibles and failures. It doesn't mean we don't see them. How many view yourself as a gifted person when it comes to seeing the faults of other people? You have an unusual ability to point out—if need be—their shortcomings. You see them very clearly. Now most of us that are like that don't see our own faults quite as well.

Gracious living doesn't mean you don't see those things—but you understand that all of us have a long way to go and you extend to others forgiveness, understanding, and grace the way you have been treated graciously by Christ. And this means we live as holy people graciously with the motive of love.

Verses 14 and 15—let's read them together:

"You must wear . . . love. Love is what binds us all together in perfect harmony. And let the peace that comes from Christ rule in your hearts. For as members of one body you are called to live in peace. And always be thankful" (NLT).

We don't need to spend a lot of money on clothes and buy hot things to wear, because the truth is that the most important thing we can wear is love. Love is what never goes out of style.

Finally, holiness means living purposefully with the power for living.

To me this call to holiness would be completely meaningless if God didn't give us the power to pull it off. Nothing is more frustrating than an invitation we can't respond to or a standard we can't achieve. But God gives us the power to become what He's calling us to be.

Look at verse 16: "Let the words of Christ, in all their richness, live in your hearts and make you wise" (NLT). What does it mean to be wise? My definition of wisdom is knowledge applied to life through understanding.

There are a lot of people that have a lot of knowledge, but they're not wise, because they don't have the understanding it takes to translate it into living. God's Word helps us do that. "Use his words to teach and counsel each other[—to] sing psalms and hymns and spiritual songs to God with thankful hearts" (NLT). And read with me verse 17: "And whatever you do or say, let it be as a representative of the Lord Jesus, all the while giving thanks through him to God the Father" (NLT).

You see, friends, holiness is more than just understanding your purpose in life. Holiness means that you have the power to fulfill it. And that's what God wants for each of us—to fulfill His purpose in our life. That's the promise of Pentecost when Christ promised in Acts 1:8, "You will receive power when the Holy Spirit comes on you; and you will be my witnesses . . . in all Judea and Samaria, and to the ends of the earth."

We will be able to pull off what God is calling us to do. Holiness is not withdrawal from the world. It's intended to make us usable for God's purpose, to make a difference in our culture. And holiness is not to be isolated and insulated from sinners. It's to be engaged in the world and to make a difference in the world. Holiness is being different to make a difference.

Let's pray together.

Lord Jesus, thank You for the clarity of Your Word and the hope of Your promise that as we surrender ourselves, You will do Your work in us.

Lord, I pray that You'll give us the courage to cut off some things from our lives that need cutting off, to get serious about what it means to pursue You, to get radical and passionate about being the people You're calling us to be—holy people.

11
CUSTODIANS
OF HOPE
SAM VASSEL

introduction and interview

During the summer 2004 Pastors and Leaders' Conferences (PALCON), over 3,000 Nazarene clergy gathered on nine Nazarene colleges/universities for a week of fellowship, learning, prayer, and the opportunity to hear some of the best Holiness preachers today.

Dr. Sam Vassel, a recent immigrant from Jamaica and pastor of the Bronx Bethany Church of the Nazarene in New York City, was invited to speak at several of the conferences. His combination of scholarly preparation, oratorical style, and passion for the Holiness tradition has been as well received among Holiness people in the United States as it has been in Jamaica.

He was a pastor communicating with peers whom he addressed as custodians of a precious tradition. Each service concluded with an extended prayer for renewal. This sermon was preached at the Southwest PALCON, on the campus of Point Loma Nazarene University, to a very receptive audience of Nazarene clergy and friends.

We talked about his message.

As a Jamaican, do you ever feel that the Holiness message is too attached to an American tradition?

I am drawn to those particular features of the Holiness message that I recognize as essential to the Holiness tradition—forgiveness of sins, purity of heart, the healing community, and compassionate engagement in the world.

You centered your message on holiness as an experience of grace.

That's right! It's the grace of forgiveness. It's the grace of the purified heart. It's the grace of community life together. It's the grace of compassion.

During the summer as I listened to your sermon, we as a church were engaged in a conversation about two divergent interpretations of holiness—that of the American Holiness Movement and that of neo-Wesleyanism. You seemed to include both of those interpretations.

I am very, very gratified that you heard it that way, because that is one of the things I wanted to do. These are some fundamental areas we can all agree on.

In a few words, how do you characterize holiness preaching?

I think Holiness preaching is the kind of preaching that proclaims a high standard of living that is attainable through grace. It is about God, the way He works. Holiness is as possible as it is necessary. One of my very good friends in Jamaica puts it this way: "Whatever God demands, He also supplies." It is therefore an optimistic message of hope.

sermon: "custodians of hope"

My friends, it has been my great honor to be asked to share in this PALCON over this summer. Time and again, God surprises us with the assignments to which He calls us. This summer I have been surprised—in the words of C. S. Lewis in his biography—"surprised by joy."

My understanding of my assignment is that PALCON seeks to reflect upon and reaffirm those things that are our core values in the Church of the Nazarene. The core values are that we are a Christian people, that we are a Holiness people, and that we are a missional people.

On Wednesday nights we seek to look at what it means to be a holiness people; the very core of the core, the distinctive of our denomination, is that we are a Holiness people. What are the essential features of this faith tradition in which we stand? I have been led to think of our faith tradition in three ways.

First, it is a faith tradition concerned with the experience of grace. Second, it is a faith tradition concerned with an experience of grace through an encounter with God—a real encounter with God. And third, it is a faith tradition concerned with a real encounter with God that will inevitably produce a real engagement in the world.

So there are three elements in this faith tradition—experiencing grace based on an encounter with God, which results in engagement in the world.

Our faith tradition is a grace tradition. It is not a tradition that is meritorious. It is a tradition that speaks about grace, because what must happen in the experience is something you do not generate yourself but something that happens to you.

Somebody has said that this tradition is concerned about something happening to people—something happens in people so that something can happen *through* people.

It is without apology a tradition that seeks God to do something in us and for us so that He can act through us in a way we can't do to ourselves, in ourselves, and for ourselves. It is preoccupied, this faith tradition, with God doing something—God doing something we can't do for ourselves. And when God does that, it is going to be clear that this is a work of God in us, to us, and through us.

So, it's a tradition that is concerned with grace. But it is a tradition that is concerned with the experience of grace—concerned not only with the description of grace, the understanding of the language of grace, but with experiencing grace. Have you experienced grace? Have you experienced grace through an encounter with God? And does this encounter with God result in your being engaged for God? And because of God, by the power of God, are you engaged in the world?

Pastors in 2004 are in a real sense the custodians of this tradition. PALCON is important because if the custodians of this tradition are persons who have not themselves *experienced* the grace—*encountered* God—and by virtue of this encounter engaged in God's world as God's people, then we are in big trouble. Because what you have is a set of people who are simply witnessing in—as I have said on occasion—a way that false witnesses witness. They are well prepared by their lawyers, they know exactly what language and words to use, but they are not *real* witnesses.

Real witnesses are persons who have experienced something and on cross-examination will therefore not be confused. On cross-examination they are not conflicted, because they have experienced something to which they bear witness.

It is so important that the custodians of the tradition, the people in the pulpit, the people leading this faith tradition, be persons who themselves are true witnesses; it is so important that they have experienced grace, that they have encountered God, and that they—as a result of their experience based upon their encounter—are engaged in the world themselves.

Perhaps there are Nazarene pastors who wonder, "What's the difference between us in the Church of the Nazarene and our friends down the road?" If the custodians of the tradition do not understand the distinctive difference, then the tradition is in trouble. The tradition runs the risk of dying with this generation. And here I want to make an important distinction between tradition and traditionalism.

Traditionalism is what results from habitual actions; it is the habitual ways of doing things and saying things that result when form is retained without essence. Traditionalism is that distasteful, insipid experience that *so* many people have of so many faith traditions. It is that thing that drives our young people away from our churches. It is that thing that kills the notion of faith as a viable way of living one's life. It is this *insipid* thing that some people call "church."

Whereas traditionalism is the dead faith of living men, tradition is the living faith of dead men. In this room tonight, we are the custodians of tradition—something that predated us. We have not invented what we are custodians of. We are the contemporary bearers of a fire that was lit before we were born, a fire passed on to us.

I don't come to the position of pastor or leader within the Holiness tradition by way of my academic study only. My own pilgrimage has been a route I have taken by means of having received the tradition. I stand as a witness in this tradition as I received it from my mother and father. And by the grace of God I want to transmit four essential things I believe define this tradition to my children and those that are following after me.

- The experience of the forgiveness of sins
- The experience of purity of heart
- The experience of a healing community
- The experience of compassionate engagement in the world

Our Holiness faith tradition—the living faith of dead men—
    is concerned with the experience of grace in the forgiveness of sins,
        concerned with the experience of grace in the purification of the heart,
            concerned with the experience of grace in being part of a healing community, and
                concerned with the experience of grace that is compassionate engagement in the world.

Brothers and sisters, I take it very seriously that we are the custodians of

this living faith of dead men. God, I believe, looked for some people nearly 100 years ago that would bear this tradition. Persons were raised up—
raised up sometimes out of churches that were supposed to be the custodians of this tradition but had become lax, had started to fail in their
duty.

And nearly 100 years ago God called people sometimes out of these
churches, called them together to form the Church of the Nazarene—
not because there needed to be another church, not because there just
had to be another church—but because God, I believe, has a vested interest that those things that are sacred in this tradition be represented
in the world.

According to our core values we are a Christian church. We are not
sectarian in the sense that we believe we are the only church. We
are very clear in recognizing that we take our place among other
Christians.

On occasion as I've talked about this, I have recognized *other*
faith traditions that have made their mark. And no doubt persons in those traditions are being faithful to God's call to being
custodians of those traditions. And I am saying that God has
called us to a particular faith tradition and that we have to be
very careful that we are faithful to our call to be custodians of
our tradition.

I am saying to us that if we do not act as faithful stewards of this tradition that is very important to God's heart, do not be surprised if we are
left simply holding the form and losing the substance.

Do not be surprised that although we may keep on having our well-
organized churches with vans and steeples and all that, God may raise
up others willing to experience grace by an encounter with Him so
that they may be engaged as His Holiness people in the world.

First, let us consider the forgiveness of sins.

We are the people who have a vision of the holy God. As a result of this
vision of a holy God, there is a preaching that is uncompromising
against sin. One of our favorite texts anywhere you go in this Holiness
tradition will be the call of Isaiah in Isa. 6:1: "I saw . . . the Lord . . . high
and lifted up" (KJV).

I would imagine that Holiness preachers in Korea, Holiness
preachers in China, Holiness preachers in Africa—all over the
world, all colors, all cultures—have gone to this text: "I saw . . . the

Lord . . . high and lifted up . . . [the] train [of his robe] filled the temple" (KJV). And there were created beings whose only task was to say, "Holy, holy, holy, is the LORD [God Almighty]: the whole earth is full of his glory" (v. 3, KJV).

And Holiness preachers, people who stand in this tradition, have heard the link made in that text over and over. When I see the Lord in His holiness, I cease to find comfort in my own complacent satisfaction by comparing myself with other people, because I suddenly realize that my comparison is with God.

And when I compare *myself* with the holy God revealed in that vision, I must cry out, "Woe is me. I am undone! I am undone because I and my contemporaries are woefully, woefully lacking in comparison to God!" (see v. 5).

It is in that light that Holiness people and Holiness preachers see sin—falling short of God's impeccable standard. It is a vision of God in which God is *absolutely flawless!* And therefore, sin—human falleness—is *starkly* evident.

The Holiness preacher, therefore, is not talking about mistakes, social deviance, and other euphemistic terms for sin. Find a Holiness preacher anywhere across the world, across the ages, and you will find somebody foaming at the mouth about sinful men in the presence of the holy God. Do you understand where I'm going? We take sin seriously.

If, however, we get to the point where Holiness preachers are saying, "Well, you know, it's really not that bad," then a tradition will have been lost. And what happens when people are no longer seeing sin as sin? They lose their vision of a holy God before whom guilty men stand!

In that story of Isaiah's call, the Holiness preacher causes condemned men to hear that the God seen in the vision is He who takes the initiative to say, "Although you are *truly* condemned, I am concerned about your conversion. I will send live coals from off the altar. And I will do in you and to you what you cannot do for yourself. I will touch you with that which comes from *Me* that will transform you and make you different" (see vv. 6-7).

So this holy God is quintessentially a merciful God, is a loving God, is a God that does what needs to be done in order to help us when we cannot help ourselves.

This is the tradition that passionately speaks to people about the possibility of being saved—saved from the consequences of sin, saved from the guilt of sin, saved from the burden of sin.

The holy God is a God not only of holy wrath and holy judgment but also of holy love and mercy. And He does what would be unthinkable in sacrificially giving His Son so that people might be saved—forgiven of their sins.

It is those people then that experience grace—the grace of the forgiveness of sin, condemned as they were—like the woman taken in the very act of adultery in the Gospel of John, for instance.

Standing before Jesus, no doubt shaking with guilt and shame because she was caught in the very act, she was going to be stoned in keeping with the holy requirements of the Law.

But she sees Jesus and hears Him saying, "I do not condemn you. Go and sin no more." One can envisage her going on her way rejoicing because she has been forgiven! (see John 8).

Or the woman in Luke 7 that sneaks into a religious party. And while they are there doing their thing, she seems to be a little antsy.

She has a box of ointment, a precious ointment, and does something that would be out of place even here in California—she breaks the box of precious ointment and pours it upon Jesus, washes His feet with her tears, and wipes them with her hair.

And Jesus, being aware that the religious group He was with did not like that open show of fanatical enthusiasm, rebuked them: "Leave her alone, for she loves much because she has been forgiven much."

Show me a tradition in which people are conscious of the forgiveness of their sins, and I will show you a tradition where worship is uninhibited. Show me a tradition where people have experienced grace in the forgiveness of sin, and I will show you a tradition where sometimes the meetings are almost chaotic with ecstatic joy.

The very heart of this tradition is the experience of grace that affirms that you can be victorious over sin, that sin does not have to reign and rule in your mortal body.

We believe that what is written in places like Rom. 6 is not just a beautiful piece of prosaic literature but a declaration that people who are dead to sin do not have to live any longer therein.

It's a tradition that tells people who are frustrated by trying harder and harder and failing that there is something God can do to you and in you that makes you a victor over sin and not a *victim* to it!

And if we don't say it, and say it with the passion of people who have had the victory ourselves through an encounter with God, then who is going to say it?

Who will God find in California in the year 2004?

Who will be able to be a witness that there is the possibility of grace—an experience of grace—based upon an encounter with God that enables you to be a victor and not a victim.

We have called this experience by various metaphorical terms. And the one I really, really am drawn to is this notion of the *purity of heart*. It is how, I believe, the Bible describes this definitive work of the Holy Spirit in the life of a believer.

And what does purity of heart entail?

Purity of heart in the theology of James is understood in the context of what he called "spiritual adultery." There can be this adultery where although you have a love relationship with God, there are other lovers.

And James in his very strident manner attacks this spiritual adultery. He writes, "Cleanse your hands, you sinners; and purify your hearts, you double-minded" (James 4:8, NKJV).

In that statement, James gives us what I believe is the essence of our Holiness tradition's understanding of the purified heart.

The purified heart is a heart that has been completely consecrated to God; it's a heart that has been drawn to and is entirely devoted to God in an undivided way; it's a heart that has no other attraction but God; it's a heart that has one desire (see Ps. 27:4).

Søren Kierkegaard, the Danish theologian, says that "purity of heart is to will one thing." When God's will and your will are in one alignment, there is no competing will. There is no competing agenda.

We assert that there can come, by the baptism of the Spirit in the life of an individual, a total selling out to God—a total surrender where God and God alone is Master of the yielded heart. That's what the Bible says. And that is what purity of heart is about.

Purity of heart is when the heart has one master, yielded to God, and that comes, in my view, in my understanding, in my reflection, not so much because of a fear of God or a fear of hell.

This purity of heart is a work that is done by the Holy Spirit where there's a vision of God's beauty. It is an encounter with the beauty of God (see Ps. 27:4).

I can reflect on my own experience. And although I do not use my experience as a definitive point of doctrine, I can witness to understanding personally what is going on. I had an experience by the Spirit where God became beautiful to me, where there was no competing beauty.

I remember after I spoke at College Church in Olathe (Kansas). A lady came and told me about her experience. In tears she said, "Yes, I remember as a college student the night I was sanctified. And what I remembered is that God became so beautiful to me that there was no competing attraction."

There is a vision of God that is more than just the holiness of God, more than just the mercy of God, more than just the love of God. There is a vision of God that is a captivating beauty.

We see nothing compared with the beauty of God, and when you see that, you want nothing else and you want nothing less. And you will tolerate nothing that will compromise that relationship with a beautiful God—you are sanctified!

I sat with my son one morning—one morning as he came in after having gone out with his friends. And I spoke to him about his faith. And my son said to me, "Daddy, I want to want God. I want to want Him."

There are people all around us who want to have a motivation from within,

a motivation that is beyond obligation,

a motivation that is beyond duty,

a motivation that comes from a grace,

a grace of having an experience with God in which God's beautiful face is revealed to them in a way that wins their heart.

That is what is at the very heart of our tradition. It is the tradition that speaks about the purity of heart.

Our tradition speaks not only about this grace of the forgiveness of sins and about this grace that is experienced in the purifying of the heart

but also about the healing community.

Go back to Wesley! He called people into his societies and from the class meetings into the bands. There were three kinds of bands.

There were the penitent bands—a nurturing community for people who were failing and kept on failing.

And there were the ordinary discipling bands where people would just have a mutual accountability to one another in the context of living the Christian life.

And there were those bands in which people who were called to ministry encouraged one another and accounted for one another as they prepared for ministry.

I am saying that it is very important to understand the place of the small group in this Holiness tradition. It is a tradition that does not do well where people are just living their lives all by themselves, in a sort of individual pietistic contemplation.

We are not a monastic sect. We are not the persons who simply celebrate that which is so wonderful about American culture—and as a non-American I say this guardedly.

You know, one of the things we non-Americans admire about Americans is a can-do attitude. Americans always feel "we can do it," "we can handle it."

Americans gave the world the Lone Ranger, and the Lone Ranger could always fix whatever problem there was all by himself, with very little help, if any, from Tonto.

But the Christian life is not a Lone Ranger thing. In fact, if you think that you can fix it and live by yourself, that is exactly where the devil wants you. For this Christian life, as pure as your heart may be, is a life that needs to be lived in community.

You need a nurturing community. You need to be able to have somebody who cares about you and is concerned about you and will pray with you and will walk with you and to whom you are accountable so that the purified heart can be nurtured and kept pure.

I was born in the mission house—right there in the churchyard—both my parents being ordained ministers. I have had 50 years to watch Holiness people. I have had a ringside seat while watching the saved and the sanctified people. And I know, having myself become a pastor, that some people are saved and sanctified, but sick nonetheless.

From the very outset, our faith tradition understood that the saved

and the sanctified needed a community that was confidential,
   a community where it was safe for confession,
      a community in which people cared for you so that that which
      is endemic and that which could become epidemic, that which
      would make saved and sanctified people sick, could be cured.
In the Bible James writes, "Is any sick among you?" (5:14, KJV). And I
don't think that that sickness must be thought of as exclusively physical sickness, because you know that many people who are really sick
are quite well physically.
   Our tradition has always had the practice of the small group holding you accountable so that your sickness can be healed.
      Confessing your faults one to another was the point in Wesley's
      band where you'd be asked four questions.
         First, "Have you sinned this week?"
            And if you did not sin, the second question was, "Were
            you tempted to sin?"
               And then the third question was, "By what?"
                  And the fourth question was, "How did you over-
                  come the temptation?" (See "Rules of the Band
                  Societies," in vol. 9 of The Works of John Wesley, Bi-
                  centennial ed.).

Can you imagine if we pastors had a support group in which we had to
answer truthfully those four questions every week? I am sure our salvation or sanctification would be in better shape than it is now.
   And friends and loved ones, the scandals of the Roman Catholic
   Church of hidden pedophiles and others who have struggled with
   sicknesses they were not able to overcome are now before the whole
   world.
      And we must not be too glib, because if we neglect our tradition of
      the healing community and do not find the context in which there
      is confidence for there to be confession and mutual care so that we
      will experience cure, then although we claim to be saved and sanc-
      tified, our church might be the focus of much scandal in the days
      and years to come.
         This is because many times there are people among us who are
         sick but have to be sick in silence—sick by themselves—for there
         is no experience of the healing community in which people can
         safely confess their faults one to another.

God's family brings us together generating these groups that care for one another. The healing community is part of our tradition, and we neglect that part of our tradition to our demise and to our detriment.

And lastly, as the people who are the custodians of this tradition, we have to be the people that are compassionately engaged in the world around us.

Those of us who have encountered God's heart are to be people who understand those things that are breaking His heart in our contemporary world. There are things that break the heart of God. Our God hears the sighs and cries of people that are oppressed. And God comes down to deliver them (see Exod. 3:7-8).

I am a man of color in the Church of the Nazarene—not because it is a place where lots of people of color are—but I am here because of my appreciation of this faith tradition.

I reflected on the voices in England that were calling out against the horrors of the Transatlantic slave trade, where expansionism led people to be willingly ignorant of the humanity of Africans—Africans whom they knew about long ago, for Egyptian society was there a long time.

It was not any credible kind of ignorance about the humanity of African people. It was the greed of European expansionism that caused even the Christian Church to sanction slavery.

And who were the voices that were raised against it in England? People like John Wesley. Wesley railed against the slave trade.

Wesley made the link between a holy God, a beautiful God, a Father God, and the heart of God. And so Wesley spoke as a man whose heart was strangely warmed, against the slave trade.

He preached against it in the same voice he preached against adultery and all other sins, so that Wilberforce could not sit in his audience without going to Parliament in England and doing everything he could until the slave trade was abolished.

In the Church of the Nazarene, even today, we are people who take a very dim view of drinking alcohol—and why? There's a historic reason we are people who don't drink alcohol.

The Church of the Nazarene started in inner-city missions where people in the face of urban drift very often went into the urban centers from their rural origins to seek work.

And when early Nazarenes saw the havoc alcohol wreaked on these people who were often frustrated, unemployed, and underemployed, they decided they would not spend one cent of their money in helping to support the destructive liquor industry.

They took a stand not to drink alcohol. And today we are the custodians of that tradition.

What is it that is happening in corporate society that is breaking the very heart of God? I've just come to live in the United States, so you know better than I.

Who are the people in the United States who are going through circumstances that break God's heart? And what is our relationship with them? Who are we standing with because God is standing with them?

Why is it that we can take in all the Cubans that can come and we let the Haitians drown in the sea? Why? Does the Church of the Nazarene care when Haiti is one of those places that, I hear, have more Nazarenes per capita than anywhere else in the world?

How do we relate to that particular policy of immigration? I'm just asking the questions.

One of my teachers said that you begin to be prophetic when you get specific. As long as you generalize, everybody will say, "Oh, that's great." But when you get specific, it becomes uncomfortable.

Who is willing to follow in the footsteps of Wesley—the man with the fire, the man with the burning heart—who made a link between the holiness of heart and the holiness of life in the compassionate engagement with people where God's heart was breaking over their voicelessness, over their disenfranchisement, over their lack of experiencing God's will for them?

I believe that persons before us have paid the price, and they have handed to us what they believed was something that captured the essence of the primitive Christian faith of the New Testament.

Sitting in this room are the persons who go to their pulpits Sunday after Sunday and are charged with being custodians of this tradition in the year 2004. And I believe that those persons who are willing to embrace that responsibility will find that the Spirit of the living God will fall afresh on them.

And by the grace of God, when God calls us on that final day, those of us who have been attending these PALCONs and have been praying through the night and have been seeking God for more than just what we've had, He will say to us—having done what He wants to do in us—"Well done, good and faithful. You have been faithful, and so I'll make you ruler over many things."

Brothers and sisters, are you with me? I wonder if you are with me. I'm going to ask you to come. Let's pray together—let's spend some time praying. Lots of things happened out here on the West Coast at the turn of the last century, and the God who did those things then has not changed. As we begin to sing, I would invite others of you to come. Let's pray together.